EVERYDAY Literacy

Science

Download Home–School Activities in Spanish

The Home–School Connection at the end of each weekly lesson in the book is also available in Spanish on our website.

How to Download:

1. Go to www.evan-moor.com/resources.

2. Enter your e-mail address and the resource code for this product—EMC5024.

3. You will receive an e-mail with a link to the downloadable letters, as well as an attachment with instructions.

Writing: Barbara Allman
Content Editing: Guadalupe Lopez
Lisa Vitarisi Mathews
Andrea Weiss
Copy Editing: Cathy Harber
Art Direction: Cheryl Puckett
Kathy Kopp
Cover Design: Cheryl Puckett
Illustration: Ruth Linstromberg
Design/Production: Carolina Caird

EMC 5024

Evan-Moor
EDUCATIONAL PUBLISHERS
Helping Children Learn since 1979

Congratulations on your purchase of some of the finest teaching materials in the world.

Correlated
to State Standards

Contents

What's Inside

In this book, you will find **20 weekly lessons**. Each weekly lesson includes:

3 Teacher Pages

Use these pages to guide you through the week.

A script to follow that introduces the science concept

A short story to read aloud to children

Daily discussion questions about the story or science concept, plus a script to guide children through the activities

A hands-on activity that reinforces the weekly concept

Samples of children's expected responses

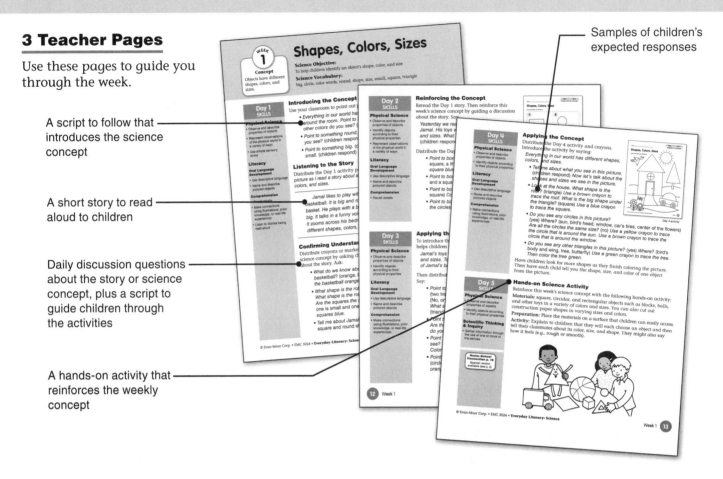

4 Student Activity Pages

Reproduce each page for children to complete during the daily lesson.

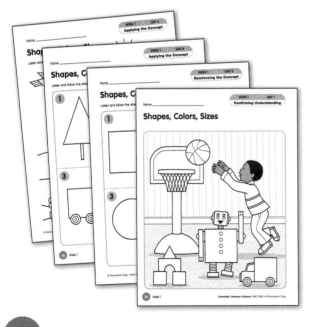

1 Home–School Connection Page

At the end of each week, give children the **Home–School Connection** page (in English or Spanish) to take home and share with their parents.

To access the Spanish version of the page, go to www.evan-moor.com/resources. Enter your e-mail address and the resource code EMC5024.

Everyday Literacy: Science • EMC 5024 • © Evan-Moor Corp.

How to Use This Book

Follow these easy steps to conduct the lessons:

Day 1

Reproduce and distribute the *Day 1 Student Page* to each child.

Use the scripted *Day 1 Teacher Page* to:

1. Introduce the weekly concept.

2. Read the story aloud as children listen and look at the picture.

3. Guide children through the activity.

Tips for Success

- Review the *Teacher Page* before you begin the lesson.

- Work with children in small groups at a table in a quiet area of the room.

- Model how to respond to questions by using complete sentences. For example, if a child responds to the question "Where does rain come from?" by answering "clouds," you'd respond, "That's right. Rain comes from the clouds."

- Wait for children to complete each task before giving the next direction.

- Provide visual aids or concrete demonstrations when possible.

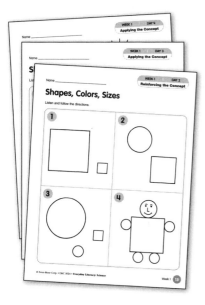

Days 2, 3, and 4

Reproduce and distribute the appropriate day's activity page to each child.

Use the scripted *Teacher Page* to:

1. Review and discuss the Day 1 story.

2. Introduce, review, or extend the science concept.

3. Guide children through the activity.

Home–School Connection

Day 5

Follow the directions to lead the Hands-on Science Activity.

Send home the **Home–School Connection** page for each child to complete with his or her parents.

Skills Chart

	Science																		
	Physical Science									Life Science						Earth Science			
Week	Observe and describe properties of objects	Represent observations of the physical world in a variety of ways	Identify objects according to their physical properties	Compare properties of objects	Understand the difference between floating and sinking	Use simple sensory terms	Understand that water can be a liquid or a solid	Become familiar with a ramp (inclined plane—simple machine)	Understand that ramps (simple machines) are used for a specific purpose	Represent observations of living things in a variety of ways	Understand that people, animals, and plants are living things that have basic needs	Identify food, water, and safe places	Understand that people, animals, and plants are living things that have parts	Understand that people, animals, and plants are living things that grow and change	Explore characteristics of living things	Represent observations about Earth and space in a variety of ways	Explore properties of Earth and space	Understand that the sun, moon, and stars are objects in our sky	Understand that the sun gives Earth light and heat
1	•	•	•			•													
2	•	•	•	•		•													
3	•	•			•														
4	•	•				•	•												
5		•						•	•										
6										•	•	•							
7										•	•								
8										•	•				•				
9										•			•		•				
10										•			•		•				
11										•			•		•				
12										•				•					
13										•				•					
14																•	•	•	•
15																•	•	•	
16																•	•	•	
17																•	•		
18																•	•		
19																•	•		
20																•	•		

Everyday Literacy: Science • EMC 5024 • © Evan-Moor Corp.

Understand that the Earth spins	Understand that the moon does not change shape	Understand that the Earth is composed of air, land, and water	Understand that the Earth has different landforms	Understand that rocks have different properties	Understand that air is everywhere	Understand that weather changes from day to day across seasons	Understand that there are different types of weather	Gather information through the use of one or more of the senses	Explore physical properties of objects and materials	Experiment with simple machines	Gather and record information through simple observations and investigations	Use descriptive language	Name and describe pictured objects	Respond orally to simple questions	Recall details	Make connections using illustrations, prior knowledge, or real-life experiences	Listen to stories being read aloud	Make inferences and draw conclusions	Week
								•				•	•		•	•	•		1
								•				•	•		•	•	•		2
									•		•	•	•		•	•	•		3
								•				•			•	•	•		4
								•	•	•		•	•		•	•	•		5
											•			•	•	•	•	•	6
								•			•			•	•	•	•	•	7
											•			•	•	•	•	•	8
								•						•	•	•	•	•	9
											•			•	•	•	•	•	10
											•			•	•	•	•	•	11
											•			•	•	•	•	•	12
								•			•			•	•	•	•	•	13
											•			•	•	•	•	•	14
•											•			•	•	•	•	•	15
	•										•			•	•	•	•	•	16
		•	•						•					•	•	•	•	•	17
		•		•							•			•	•	•	•	•	18
		•			•						•			•	•	•	•	•	19
						•	•				•	•		•	•	•	•	•	20

Everyday Literacy
Science

Student Progress Record

Name: _____

Write dates and comments in the boxes below the student's proficiency level.

1: Rarely demonstrates   0 – 25%
2: Occasionally demonstrates 25 – 50%
3: Usually demonstrates   50 – 75%
4: Consistently demonstrates 75 – 100%

Pre-Literacy Concepts

	1	2	3	4
Communicates using drawing and tracing				
Tracks print and pictures from top to bottom and left to right				
Understands that pictures and symbols have meaning and that print carries a message				

Oral Language Development

Uses descriptive language				
Names and describes pictured objects				
Responds orally to simple questions				

Comprehension

Recalls details				
Makes connections using illustrations, prior knowledge, or real-life experiences				
Listens to stories being read aloud				
Makes inferences and draws conclusions				

Science

Uses content vocabulary when speaking				
Engages in scientific thinking and inquiry				

Everyday Literacy
Science

PreK

Small-Group Record Sheet

Students' Names:

Write dates and comments about students' performance each week.

Week	Title	Comments
1	Shapes, Colors, Sizes	
2	Alike or Different?	
3	Float or Sink?	
4	Water and Ice	
5	Up the Ramp	
6	What Animals Need	
7	What People Need	
8	What Plants Need	
9	Our Bodies Have Parts	
10	Plants Have Parts	
11	Animals Have Parts	
12	Living and Nonliving Things	
13	People Grow and Change	
14	We Need the Sun	
15	Day and Night	
16	The Moon	
17	The Earth Has Land	
18	All Kinds of Rocks	
19	Air Is Everywhere	
20	How's the Weather?	

Dear Parent or Guardian,

Every week your child will learn a concept that focuses on Physical, Life, or Earth Science. Your child will develop oral language and comprehension skills by listening to stories and engaging in oral, written, and hands-on activities that reinforce science concepts.

At the end of each week, I will send home an activity page for you to complete with your child. The activity page reviews the weekly science concept and has an activity for you and your child to do together.

Sincerely,

Estimado padre o tutor:

Cada semana su niño(a) aprenderá sobre un concepto de ciencias físicas, naturales o de la Tierra. Su niño(a) desarrollará las habilidades de lenguaje oral y de comprensión escuchando cuentos y realizando actividades orales y escritas. Además, participará en actividades prácticas que apoyan los conceptos de ciencias.

Al final de cada semana, le enviaré una hoja de actividades para que la complete en casa con su niño(a). La hoja repasa el concepto científico de la semana, y contiene una actividad que pueden completar usted y su niño(a) juntos.

Atentamente,

Shapes, Colors, Sizes

Science Objective:
To help children identify an object's shape, color, and size

Science Vocabulary:
big, circle, color words, round, shape, size, small, square, triangle

Day 1 SKILLS

Physical Science
- Observe and describe properties of objects
- Represent observations of the physical world in a variety of ways
- Use simple sensory terms

Literacy

Oral Language Development
- Use descriptive language
- Name and describe pictured objects

Comprehension
- Recall details
- Make connections using illustrations, prior knowledge, or real-life experiences
- Listen to stories being read aloud

Introducing the Concept

Use your classroom to point out properties of objects. Say:

- *Everything in our world has different shapes, colors, and sizes. Look around the room. Point to something blue.* (children respond) *What other colors do you see?* (children respond)

- *Point to something round.* (children respond) *What other shapes do you see?* (children respond)

- *Point to something big.* (children respond) *Now point to something small.* (children respond)

Listening to the Story

Distribute the Day 1 activity page to each child. Say: *Listen and look at the picture as I read a story about a boy who has toys that are different shapes, colors, and sizes.*

Jamal likes to play with his toys. He plays with an orange basketball. It is big and round. Jamal tries to throw the ball into the basket. He plays with a blue robot. Its head is small and its body is big. It talks in a funny voice. Jamal plays with his small green truck. It zooms across his bedroom floor. Jamal plays with toys that are all different shapes, colors, and sizes.

Confirming Understanding

Distribute crayons or markers. Develop the science concept by asking children questions about the story. Ask:

- *What do we know about Jamal's basketball?* (orange, big, round) *Color the basketball orange.*

- *What shape is the robot's head?* (square) *What shape is the robot's body?* (square) *Are the squares the same size?* (No, one is small and one is big.) *Color the squares blue.*

- *Tell me about Jamal's truck.* (small, has square and round shapes) *Color the truck green.*

Day 1 picture

Day 2
SKILLS

Physical Science
- Observe and describe properties of objects
- Identify objects according to their physical properties
- Represent observations of the physical world in a variety of ways

Literacy

Oral Language Development
- Use descriptive language
- Name and describe pictured objects

Comprehension
- Recall details

Reinforcing the Concept

Reread the Day 1 story. Then reinforce this week's science concept by guiding a discussion about the story. Say:

Yesterday we read a story about a boy named Jamal. His toys were different shapes, colors, and sizes. What shapes were his toys? (children respond)

Distribute the Day 2 activity and crayons. Say:

- *Point to box 1. What do you see?* (a big square, a little square) *Color the big square blue.*
- *Point to box 2. What do you see?* (a circle and a square) *Color the square red.*
- *Point to box 3. What do you see?* (a big circle, a small circle, and a small square) *Color the big circle yellow. Color the small circle orange.*
- *Point to box 4. What shapes do you see?* (square and circles) *Are all the circles the same size?* (no) *Color the circles green.*

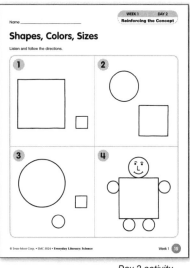

Day 2 activity

Day 3
SKILLS

Physical Science
- Observe and describe properties of objects
- Identify objects according to their physical properties

Literacy

Oral Language Development
- Use descriptive language
- Name and describe pictured objects

Comprehension
- Make connections using illustrations, prior knowledge, or real-life experiences

Applying the Concept

To introduce the activity, guide a discussion that helps children recall the Day 1 story. Say:

Jamal's toys were all different shapes, colors, and sizes. Tell me about the shape and size of Jamal's basketball. (children respond)

Then distribute the Day 3 activity and crayons. Say:

- *Point to picture 1. What do you see?* (two trees) *Are the trees the same size?* (No, one is big/tall and one is small/short.) *What shapes are the tops of the trees?* (triangles) *Color the big triangle green.*
- *Point to picture 2. What do you see?* (birds) *Are they the same size?* (No, one is small and one is big.) *What shapes do you see?* (triangles and circles) *Color the small bird yellow.*
- *Point to picture 3. What do you see?* (a truck) *What shapes do you see?* (squares and circles) *Are all the squares the same size?* (no) *Color the squares blue.*
- *Point to picture 4. What do you see?* (balls) *What shape are they?* (circles/round) *Are all the balls the same size?* (no) *Color the big ball orange. Color the medium ball yellow. Color the small ball purple.*

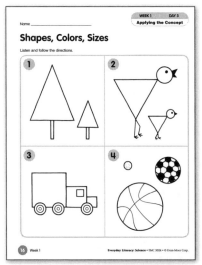

Day 3 activity

Applying the Concept

Distribute the Day 4 activity and crayons. Introduce the activity by saying:

Everything in our world has different shapes, colors, and sizes.

- *Tell me about what you see in this picture.* (children respond) *Now let's talk about the shapes and sizes we see in the picture.*

- *Look at the house. What shape is the roof?* (triangle) *Use a brown crayon to trace the roof. What is the big shape under the triangle?* (square) *Use a blue crayon to trace the square.*

- *Do you see any circles in this picture?* (yes) *Where?* (sun, bird's head, window, car's tires, center of the flowers) *Are all the circles the same size?* (no) *Use a yellow crayon to trace the circle that is around the sun. Use a brown crayon to trace the circle that is around the window.*

- *Do you see any other triangles in this picture?* (yes) *Where?* (bird's body and wing, tree, butterfly) *Use a green crayon to trace the tree. Then color the tree green.*

Have children look for more shapes as they finish coloring the picture. Then have each child tell you the shape, size, and color of one object from the picture.

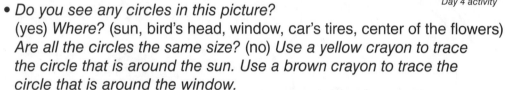
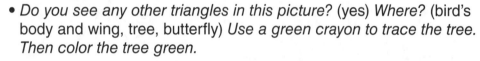

Day 4 activity

Hands-on Science Activity

Reinforce this week's science concept with the following hands-on activity:

Materials: square, circular, and rectangular objects such as blocks, balls, and other toys in a variety of colors and sizes. You can also cut out construction paper shapes in varying sizes and colors.

Preparation: Place the materials on a surface that children can easily access.

Activity: Explain to children that they will each choose an object and then tell their classmates about its color, size, and shape. They might also say how it feels (e.g., rough or smooth).

Name _____

Shapes, Colors, Sizes

Shapes, Colors, Sizes

Listen and follow the directions.

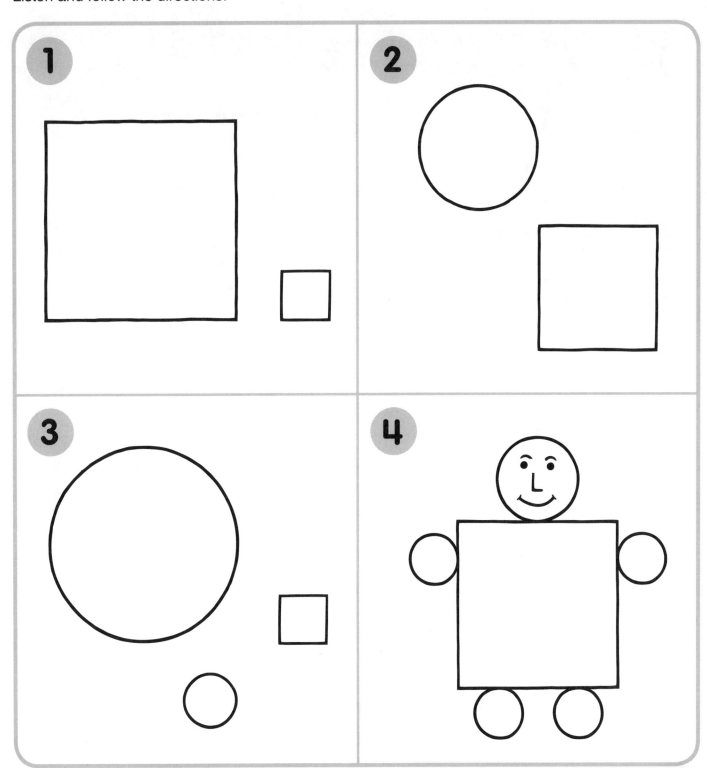

Name _____

Shapes, Colors, Sizes

Listen and follow the directions.

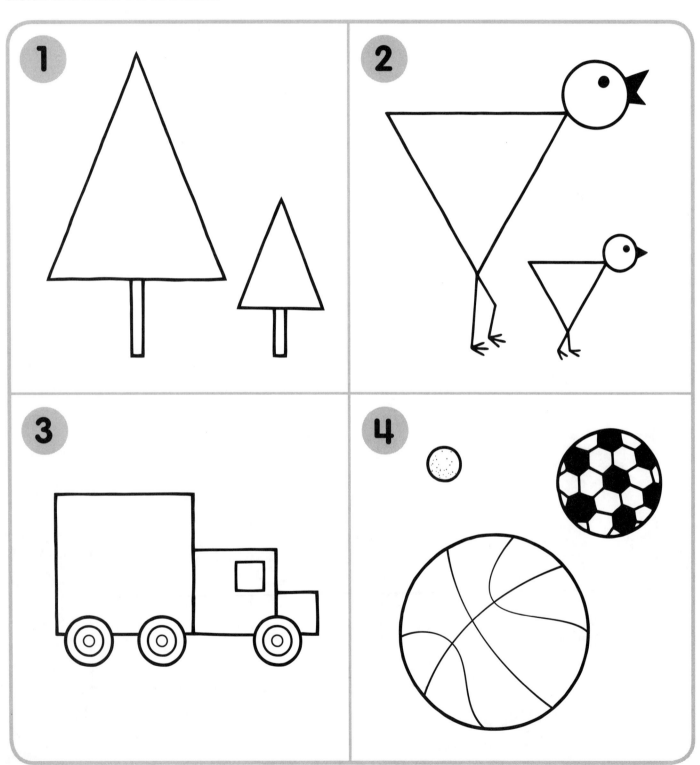

Name _____

Shapes, Colors, Sizes

Listen and follow the directions.

Name _____

What I Learned

What to Do
Look at the picture below with your child. Talk about the different shapes and sizes of the objects. Then have your child color the picture and tell you each object's color.

Science Concept: Objects have different shapes, colors, and sizes.

To Parents
This week your child learned that objects have different shapes, colors, and sizes.

What to Do Next
Ask your child to find an object that has a particular shape, color, or size. For example, say: *Find an object that is small.* or *Find an object that is blue.* Then invite your child to ask you to find objects of different shapes, sizes, and colors.

Alike or Different?

Science Objective:
To help children understand that objects have characteristics that make
them alike and different

Science Vocabulary:
alike, big, circle, color words, different, shape, size, small, square, triangle

Day 1
SKILLS

Physical Science

• Observe and describe
properties of objects

• Represent observations
of the physical world in
a variety of ways

• Compare properties
of objects

• Use simple sensory
terms

Literacy

**Oral Language
Development**

• Use descriptive language

• Name and describe
pictured objects

Comprehension

• Recall details

• Make connections
using illustrations, prior
knowledge, or real-life
experiences

• Listen to stories being
read aloud

Introducing the Concept

Use your classroom environment to compare properties of objects. Say:
Everything in our world has a shape, a color, and a size.

• *Some things look alike. Find two things in the room that have
the same color.* (children respond)

• *Some things look different. Find two things in the room that are
a different shape.* (children respond)

Listening to the Story

Distribute the Day 1 activity page to each child. Say: *Listen and look at the
picture as I read about a boy who has stickers that are alike and different.*

---

*Troy has a lot of stickers. He has stickers that are squares. The
squares are red. Some are big and some are small. Troy has stickers
that are circles. The circles are blue. Some are big and some are
small. Troy has stickers that are triangles. They are all green. They
are all small. Troy's stickers are different shapes, colors, and sizes.
In some ways they are alike, and in some ways they are different.*

Confirming Understanding

Distribute crayons or markers. Reinforce the
science concept by asking children questions
about the story. Ask:

Day 1 picture

• *How are the square stickers different from
each other?* (Some are big and some are
small.) *Make a red dot on the squares that
are big.*

• *In the story, how are all the squares alike?*
(They are red.) *Color the small square
stickers red.*

• *Are all the circle stickers the same size?*
(No, some are big and some are small.)
*Make a blue dot on the small circles.
Color the big circles blue.*

• *How are all the triangle stickers alike?* (They are all the same size.)
Color the triangles green.

Physical Science
- Observe and describe properties of objects
- Identify objects according to their physical properties
- Represent observations of the physical world in a variety of ways

Literacy

Oral Language Development
- Use descriptive language
- Name and describe pictured objects

Comprehension
- Recall details

Reinforcing the Concept

Reread the Day 1 story. Then reinforce this week's science concept by guiding a discussion about the story. Say:

- *Tell me one thing that was the same about some of the stickers.* (shape, size)

- *Tell me one thing that was different. Allow children to color the happy or sad face each time for asking the next question.* (shape, size, color)

Distribute the Day 2 activity and crayons. Allow children to color the happy or sad face each time before asking the next question. Say:

- *Point to box 1. Are the shapes the same size? Color the happy face for **yes** or the sad face for **no**.* (no) *How are the shapes different from each other?* (Some are big and some are small.)

- *Point to box 2. Are all the shapes circles? Color the happy face for **yes** or the sad face for **no**.* (yes) *Are all the circles the same size?* (no)

- *Point to box 3. Are all the shapes alike? Color the happy face for **yes** or the sad face for **no**.* (yes) *How are they alike?* (They are the same shape and size.) *What shape are they?* (triangle)

- *Point to box 4. Are all the shapes different? Color the happy face for **yes** or the sad face for **no**.* (yes) *How are they different?* (one triangle, one square, one circle)

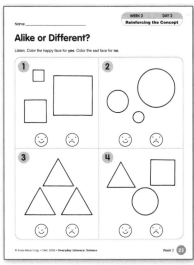

Day 2 activity

Physical Science
- Observe and describe properties of objects
- Identify objects according to their physical properties

Literacy

Oral Language Development
- Use descriptive language
- Name and describe pictured objects

Applying the Concept

Distribute the Day 3 activity and crayons. Then introduce the activity by saying:

- *Point to row 1. Look at all the balls. Find the ball that is different and circle it. How is it different?* (It is smaller.)

- *Point to row 2. Look at all the kites. Find the kite that is different and circle it. How is it different?* (It has a different color.)

- *Point to row 3. Look at all the shapes. Find the shape that is different and circle it. How is it different?* (It is a heart shape, not a star shape.)

- *Point to row 4. Look at all the robots. Find the robot that is different and circle it. How is it different?* (Its head is a square instead of a circle.)

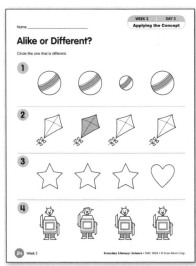

Day 3 activity

Physical Science

• Observe and describe properties of objects

• Identify objects according to their physical properties

Literacy

Oral Language Development

• Use descriptive language

• Name and describe pictured objects

Comprehension

• Make connections using illustrations, prior knowledge, or real-life experiences

Applying the Concept

Show children three crayons, two of the same color or size. Then say:

Objects can be alike and different.

• *Point to the two crayons that are alike.* (children respond) *Tell me how they are alike.* (children respond)

• *Point to the two crayons that are different.* (children respond) *How are they different?* (children respond)

Distribute the Day 4 activity and crayons. Say:

• *Look at row 1. Point to the first picture. What is it?* (a house) *Now look at the picture next to it. It looks different. What shape is missing?* (triangle; roof) *Draw the missing triangle to make the houses the same.*

• *Look at row 2. Point to the first picture. What is it?* (a flower) *Now look at the picture next to it. It looks different. What shape is missing?* (circle) *Draw the missing circle to make the flowers the same.*

• *Look at row 3. Point to the first picture. What is it?* (a robot) *Now look at the picture next to it. It looks different. What shape is missing?* (square) *Draw the missing square to make the robots look alike.*

• *Look at row 4. Point to the first picture. What is it?* (a balloon) *Now look at the picture next to it. What is different?* (the color) *Color the balloon to make the balloons look alike.*

Day 4 activity

Hands-on Science Activity

Reinforce this week's science concept with the following hands-on activity:

Materials: colorful sidewalk chalk, at least two beanbags, and a sidewalk or paved area

Preparation: Use the chalk to draw several triangles, squares, and circles of various sizes and colors on a paved area. Be sure to draw a match for each shape.

Activity: Give each child an opportunity to toss the beanbags onto two shapes. The child then calls out "alike" or "different" to describe the shapes the beanbags land on. He or she should also say what is alike or different— the color, shape, or size.

Extend the Lesson: Call out "alike" or "different" first, then have children toss the beanbags onto two shapes that illustrate what you said.

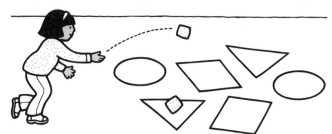

Home–School Connection p. 26
Spanish version available (see p. 2)

Name _____

Alike or Different?

Everyday Literacy: Science • EMC 5024 • © Evan-Moor Corp.

Name _____

Alike or Different?

Listen. Color the happy face for **yes**. Color the sad face for **no**.

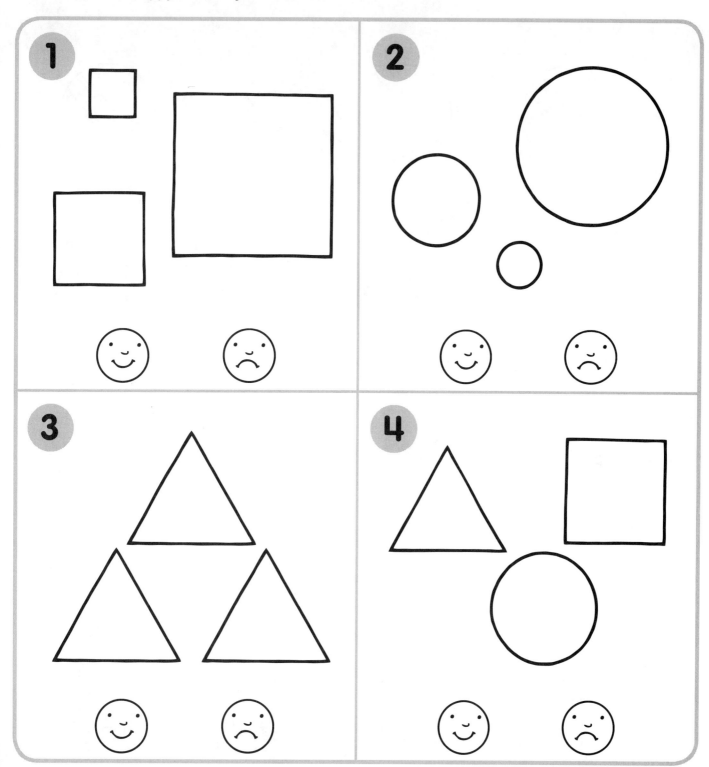

Name _____

Alike or Different?

Circle the one that is different.

1

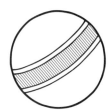 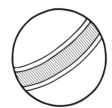 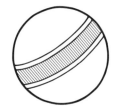

2

 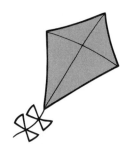  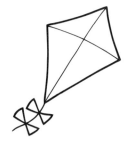

3

4

Name _____

Alike or Different?

Listen and follow the directions.

1

 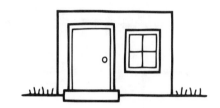

2

3

 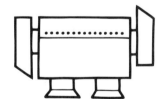

4

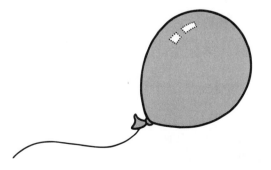 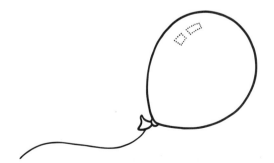

Name _____

What I Learned

What to Do
Have your child look at the shapes below and name them.
Then ask your child to color all the squares red, all the circles
blue, and all the triangles green. Discuss how the shapes are
alike and different.

Science Concept: Objects
can be alike and different.

To Parents
This week your child learned
that objects can be alike and
different.

What to Do Next
Cut squares, triangles, and circles of various sizes from different-colored paper. Then help your
child sort them, matching the ones that are alike in size, shape, and color.

Everyday Literacy: Science • EMC 5024 • © Evan-Moor Corp.

Float or Sink?

WEEK 3

Concept
Some things float and some things sink.

Science Objective:
To help children understand the difference between floating and sinking

Science Vocabulary:
bottom, float, sink/sank, top

Physical Science
- Observe and describe properties of objects
- Represent observations of the physical world in a variety of ways
- Understand the difference between floating and sinking

Literacy

Oral Language Development
- Use descriptive language
- Name and describe pictured objects

Comprehension
- Recall details
- Make connections using illustrations, prior knowledge, or real-life experiences
- Listen to stories being read aloud

Introducing the Concept

Introduce children to the concept of observing and describing what objects do when you place them in water. Say:

When you place an object in water, it floats on the water or it sinks to the bottom of the water.

- *Have you ever put a toy into the bathtub?* (children respond)
- *Did the toy stay on top of the water and float, or did it sink to the bottom of the water?* (children respond)

Listening to the Story

Distribute the Day 1 activity page to each child. Say: *Listen and look at the picture as I read a story about objects that float or sink in water.*

Miss Laura gave Ava and Jesse a tub of water, a toy boat, and a penny and said, "We're going to find out what floats and what sinks."

First, Ava dropped the boat into the water and watched for a minute. "It floats!" said Ava.

Then Jesse dropped the penny into the water and watched. "It sank to the bottom!" said Jesse.

"Some things float and some things sink," said Miss Laura. "Now put these other things into the water, one at a time. Watch and see which objects float and which objects sink."

Confirming Understanding

Distribute crayons or markers. Reinforce the science concept by asking children questions about the story. Ask:

- *What does it mean when something **floats**?* (It stays on top of the water.) *Look at the picture. Which objects are floating?* (feather, boat, leaf) *Circle all the things that are **floating**.*

- *What does it mean when something **sinks**?* (It goes to the bottom of the water.) *Look at the picture. Which objects sank?* (penny, toy car, shell) *Make a blue dot on all of the things that **sank**.*

Day 1 picture

Physical Science

- Observe and describe properties of objects
- Represent observations of the physical world in a variety of ways
- Understand the difference between floating and sinking

Literacy

Oral Language Development

- Use descriptive language

Comprehension

- Recall details
- Make connections using illustrations, prior knowledge, or real-life experiences

Reinforcing the Concept

Reinforce this week's science concept by guiding a discussion about the Day 1 story. Say:

Yesterday we learned that some things float and some things sink. Why were Ava and Jesse putting things into a tub of water? (to find out what floats and what sinks)

Distribute the Day 2 activity and crayons. Guide children in locating the **float** and **sink** icons that they will circle. Say:

- *Look at the tub of water at the top of the page. Some things are floating and some things sank to the bottom.*

- *Point to box 1. Did the ball float or sink?* (float) *Circle the picture that shows* **float**.

- *Point to box 2. Did the spoon float or sink?* (sink) *Circle the picture that shows* **sink**.

- *Point to box 3. Did the car float or sink?* (sink) *Circle the picture that shows* **sink**.

- *Point to box 4. Did the duck float or sink?* (float) *Circle the picture that shows* **float**.

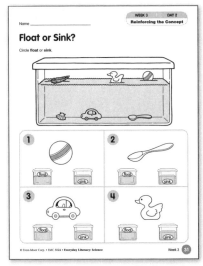

Day 2 activity

Physical Science

- Observe and describe properties of objects
- Represent observations of the physical world in a variety of ways
- Understand the difference between floating and sinking

Literacy

Oral Language Development

- Use descriptive language

Comprehension

- Make connections using illustrations, prior knowledge, or real-life experiences

Applying the Concept

Introduce the activity by saying:

You can see if something floats or sinks in a swimming pool, a fishbowl, a lake, or even in a glass of water.

- *Can you think of something you've seen that was floating? What was it? Where was it?* (children respond)

Distribute the Day 3 activity and crayons. Say:

- *Look at box 1. Is the boat in the picture floating? Color the happy face for* **yes** *or the sad face for* **no**. (yes) *Have you ever been in a boat?* (children respond)

- *Look at box 2. Is the ice cube floating? Color the happy face for* **yes** *or the sad face for* **no**. (yes) *Where else have you seen ice floating?* (children respond)

- *Look at box 3. Are the shells floating? Color the happy face for* **yes** *or the sad face for* **no**. (no) *What did the shells do?* (They sank.)

- *Look at box 4. Is the girl floating? Color the happy face for* **yes** *or the sad face for* **no**. (yes) *Have you ever floated? Where?* (children respond)

Day 3 activity

Physical Science

• Observe and describe properties of objects

• Represent observations of the physical world in a variety of ways

• Understand the difference between floating and sinking

Literacy

Comprehension

• Make connections using illustrations, prior knowledge, or real-life experiences

Applying the Concept

Distribute the Day 4 activity and crayons. Say:

• *Look at the picture at the top of the page. Listen to this story: One day, Lucy went to the dock. She threw a rock into the water. It made a big splash and sank to the bottom of the water.*

• *Now look at the pictures at the bottom of the page. Which picture shows what happened first?* (Lucy throwing rock into the water) *Draw a line from the number 1 to that picture.*

• *Which picture shows what happened second?* (rock hitting water and making a splash) *Draw a line from the number 2 to that picture.*

• *Which picture shows what happened third?* (rock sank to bottom of the water) *Draw a line from the number 3 to that picture.*

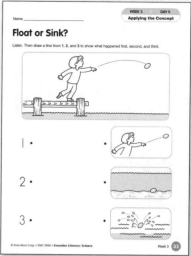

Day 4 activity

Home–School Connection p. 34
Spanish version available (see p. 2)

Hands-on Science Activity

Reinforce this week's science concept with the following hands-on activity:

Materials: clear plastic tubs or other containers to hold water

Preparation: Set up an experiment center that includes tubs of water and common items such as leaves, blocks, coins, small toys, utensils, etc. Make a two-column chart on the board or an easel to record which items float and which items sink.

Activity: Model how to put items into the water and watch them long enough to see if they float or sink. Then record the results as a class. Allow each child to have a turn placing an item into the water, observing, and recording.

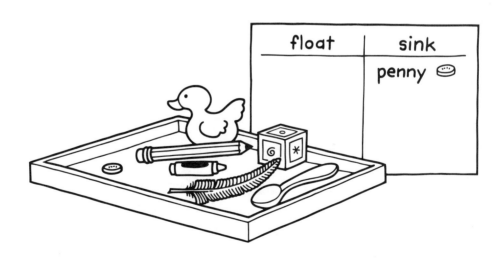

Float or Sink?

Name _____

Float or Sink?

Circle **float** or **sink**.

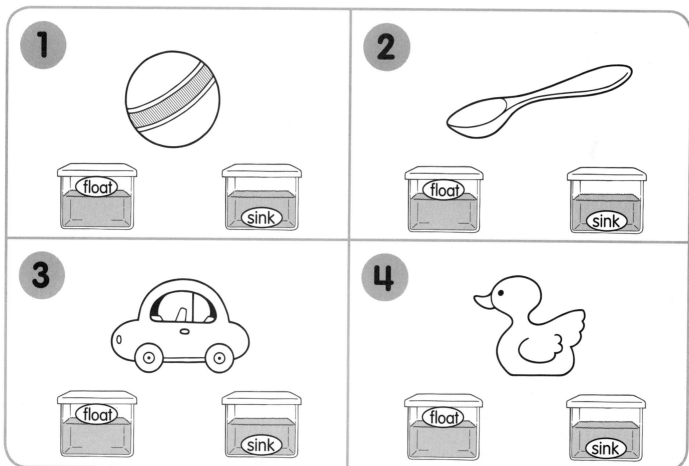

Name _____

Float or Sink?

Is it floating? Color the happy face for **yes**. Color the sad face for **no**.

Name _____

Float or Sink?

Listen. Then draw a line from **1**, **2**, and **3** to show what happened first, second, and third.

1 •	• 
2 •	• 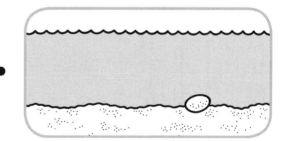
3 •	• 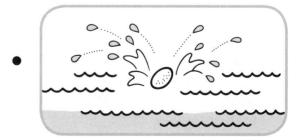

Name _____

What I Learned

What to Do

Ask your child to explain what it means when something floats (It's on top of the water) and when something sinks (It goes to the bottom of the water). Then look at the picture with your child and have him or her point out which objects are floating and which objects sank.

Science Concept: Some things float and some things sink.

To Parents
This week your child learned that some things float and some things sink.

What to Do Next

Help your child conduct a simple experiment to see which objects float and which objects sink. Fill the kitchen sink or bathtub with water and place objects in the water one at a time. Make predictions about which objects will float and which will sink.

Concept

A liquid can freeze and become a solid.

Water and Ice

Science Objective:

To help children understand that ice is the solid form of liquid water

Science Vocabulary:

freeze/frozen, ice, liquid, melt, pour, solid

Day 1 SKILLS

Physical Science

- Observe and describe properties of objects
- Use simple sensory terms
- Understand that water can be a liquid or a solid

Literacy

Oral Language Development

- Use descriptive language

Comprehension

- Recall details
- Make connections using illustrations, prior knowledge, or real-life experiences
- Listen to stories being read aloud

Introducing the Concept

Before the lesson, freeze a paper cup of water. During the lesson, display the frozen cup of water beside a paper cup filled with water. Say:

When water gets very, very cold, it freezes and becomes ice. The water starts as a liquid and becomes a solid.

Allow children to touch the ice. Ask:

- *How does the ice feel?* (cold, hard, slippery) *Does the ice move?* (no)

Then allow children to dip their fingers into the cup of water. Ask:

- *How does the water feel?* (wet, not as cold) *Does the water move?* (yes)

Listening to the Story

Distribute the Day 1 activity page to each child. Say: *I'm going to read a story that explains how water changes when it gets very cold.*

Ella lives near a pond. In the summer, when it's warm, she swims in the pond. She jumps into the water and splashes around. When winter comes, the weather gets very cold. The water in the pond freezes and becomes ice. Ella touches the ice with her hand. It feels cold and hard. The pond is frozen solid. Ella cannot swim in the water, so she finds another way to have fun—she puts on her ice skates and glides across the ice!

Confirming Understanding

Distribute crayons or markers. Develop the science concept by asking children questions about the story. Ask:

- *How did Ella play in the pond during the summer?* (swim, jump, splash) *Make a green dot on the pond water.*

- *How did the pond water change in the winter?* (became a solid; froze into ice) *What made it freeze?* (the cold)

- *How did the ice feel when Ella touched it?* (cold, hard) *Make a blue dot on the frozen pond.*

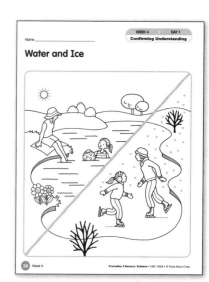

Day 1 picture

Physical Science

- Observe and describe properties of objects
- Use simple sensory terms
- Understand that water can be a liquid or a solid

Literacy

Oral Language Development

- Use descriptive language

Comprehension

- Recall details
- Make connections using illustrations, prior knowledge, or real-life experiences

Reinforcing the Concept

Reread the Day 1 story. Then reinforce this week's science concept. Say:

In the story we read, the pond changed. During the cold winter, it froze into ice and became a solid. During the warm summer, the pond melted and became water again.

Distribute the Day 2 activity and crayons. Say:

- *Listen to this story: One day a boy made ice cubes. First, he poured water into the ice cube tray. Second, he placed the tray in the freezer. Then he waited for a day. Finally, he took the tray out of the freezer. It had ice cubes in it! He put the ice cubes in a glass.*

- *What did the boy do first?* (poured water into the ice cube tray) *Put your finger on the number 1. Draw a line from the number 1 to the picture that shows the boy pouring water.*

- *What did the boy do second?* (placed the tray in the freezer) *Put your finger on the number 2. Draw a line from the number 2 to that picture.*

- *What did the boy do the next day?* (took out the tray and put ice cubes in a glass) *Put your finger on the number 3. Draw a line from the number 3 to the picture that shows the boy putting ice cubes in a glass.*

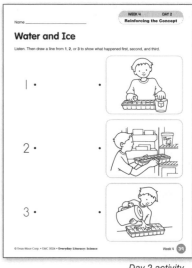

Day 2 activity

Physical Science

- Observe and describe properties of objects
- Use simple sensory terms
- Understand that water can be a liquid or a solid

Literacy

Oral Language Development

- Use descriptive language

Comprehension

- Make connections using illustrations, prior knowledge, or real-life experiences

Identifying the Concept

To introduce the activity, say:

When water is able to be poured, we call it a liquid. When water is frozen hard, we call it ice. Ice is a solid. What do you think happens when ice melts? (goes back to being a liquid)

Distribute the Day 3 activity and crayons. Say:

- *Put your finger on picture 1. It shows ice cubes in a glass. The sun came out and melted the ice. The solid ice cubes turned into a liquid water. Which picture shows that?* (water in the glass) *Draw a line to that picture.*

Day 3 activity

- *Put your finger on picture 2. These are frozen icicles on a house. It was a sunny, warm day and the icicles melted. Which picture shows what happened?* (children respond) *Draw a line to that picture.*

- *Put your finger on picture 3. This is a snowman. When the sun came out, the snowman melted. Which picture shows what happened?* (children respond) *Draw a line to that picture.*

- *Put your finger on picture 4. This is a frozen juice bar. Which picture shows what happened to it on a hot day?* (children respond) *Draw a line to that picture.*

Physical Science
- Observe and describe properties of objects
- Use simple sensory terms
- Understand that water can be a liquid or a solid

Literacy

Oral Language Development
- Use descriptive language

Comprehension
- Make connections using illustrations, prior knowledge, or real-life experiences

Applying the Concept

Introduce the activity by reviewing the following concept. Say:

Water is a liquid that you can pour. When water freezes, it changes to ice. Ice is a solid. When it melts, it changes back into water.

Distribute the Day 4 activity and crayons. Say:

- *Point to box 1. The pictures show a snowman, a scarf, and a skate. Which one is frozen?* (snowman) *Make a blue circle around the snowman.*

- *Point to box 2. The pictures show an apple, a hot dog, and a snow cone. Which one is made of ice?* (snow cone) *What would happen to a snow cone on a hot day?* (It would melt.) *Make an orange circle around the snow cone.*

- *Point to box 3. The pictures show an egg, a leaf, and some icicles. Which one is frozen solid?* (icicles) *If you touched them, how do you think they would feel?* (cold) *Make a green circle around the icicles.*

- *Point to box 4. The pictures show an ice cube, a strawberry, and a banana. Which one is changing to water?* (ice cube) *Make a black circle around the ice cube.*

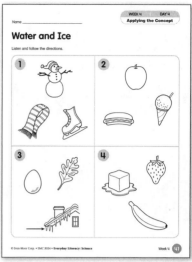

Day 4 activity

Physical Science
- Observe and describe properties of objects
- Represent observations of the physical world in a variety of ways
- Understand that water can be liquid or solid

Scientific Thinking & Inquiry
- Gather information through the use of one or more of the senses

Home–School Connection p. 42
Spanish version available (see p. 2)

Hands-on Science Activity

Reinforce this week's science concept with the following hands-on activity:

Materials: ice cubes, a bowl of very warm water, and a bowl of very cold water

Activity: Set up the water bowls where children can access them. Allow the children to dip their fingers into the bowls to feel the difference in temperature. Say:

You know that ice cubes are frozen water and that they can melt. I'm going to place one ice cube in warm water and one in cold water. Can you guess which one will melt first? (children respond)

Have children observe what happens to the ice cubes. Then ask:

Which one melted faster? (the one in warm water) *What makes ice melt?* (when it gets warm) *The ice cube in the warm water got warmer quicker than the ice cube in the cold water.*

Name _____

Water and Ice

Everyday Literacy: Science • EMC 5024 • © Evan-Moor Corp.

Name _____

Water and Ice

Listen. Then draw a line from **1**, **2**, and **3** to show what happened first, second, and third.

1 •   •

2 •   •

3 •   •

Name _____

Water and Ice

Listen. Draw a line to match.

1  • •

2  • •

3  • •

4  • •

Name _____

Water and Ice

Listen and follow the directions.

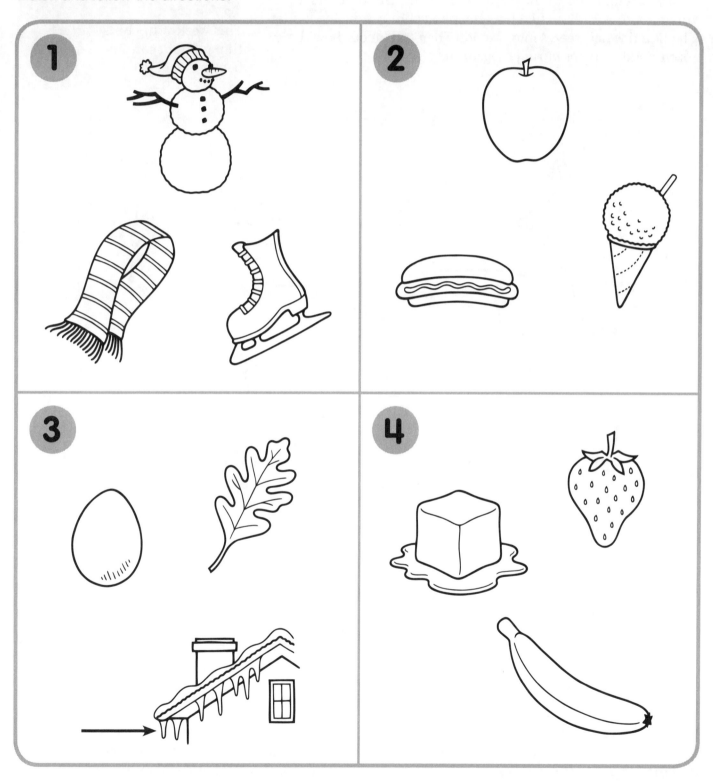

Name _____

What I Learned

What to Do
Have your child look at the pictures of a summer pond and a winter pond. Ask your child how the pond changes during winter. (The liquid water freezes into a solid.) Then talk about how the frozen pond changes during the summer.

Home–School Connection

Science Concept: A liquid can freeze and become a solid.

To Parents
This week your child learned that a liquid can freeze and become a solid.

What to Do Next
Give your child two ice cubes to place on plates. Ask your child to put one plate in a sunny place and the other in a shady place. Observe the ice cubes to see if one melts quicker than the other.

Everyday Literacy: Science • EMC 5024 • © Evan-Moor Corp.

Concept

A ramp is easier to go up and down than stairs are.

Up the Ramp

Science Objective:

To introduce children to the idea that a ramp makes work easier for people

Science Vocabulary:

pull, push, ramp, stairs, work

Day 1 SKILLS

Physical Science

- Represent observations of the physical world in a variety of ways
- Become familiar with a ramp (inclined plane—simple machine)
- Understand that ramps (simple machines) are used for a specific purpose

Literacy

Oral Language Development

- Use descriptive language

Comprehension

- Recall details
- Make connections using illustrations, prior knowledge, or real-life experiences
- Listen to stories being read aloud

Introducing the Concept

Distribute the Day 1 activity page to each child and point to the picture of the ramp. Say:

This is a ramp. Many buildings that have stairs have ramps, too. The ramps make it easier for people to get into buildings. Ramps are easier to use than stairs. Ramps make work easier.

- *Have you ever seen or used a ramp?* (children respond)

Help children think of places that often have a ramp. (e.g., stores, schools, office buildings, etc.)

Listening to the Story

Redirect children's attention to the Day 1 page. Say: *Listen and look at the picture as I read a story about a family who uses a ramp to make work easier.*

Tiffany and Sara want to bring all of their blocks into the house. Tiffany and Sara stack the blocks in their red wagon. Then they pull the wagon to the bottom of the stairs. They look at the stairs and wonder how they will pull the wagon up the stairs. They need help solving this problem. Their dad offers to help them. He gets a flat board and places it over the stairs to make a ramp. "Now you can pull the wagon up the ramp," he says. The girls pull the wagon up the ramp. It makes the work of moving the blocks much easier.

Confirming Understanding

Distribute crayons or markers. Reinforce the science concept by asking children questions about the story. Ask:

- *What work did the girls do at the beginning of the story?* (They put their blocks into the wagon.) *Circle the wagon full of blocks.*

- *What problem did the girls have?* (They needed to get the wagon full of blocks up the stairs.) *Make a red dot on the stairs.*

- *How did their dad help solve the problem?* (He made a ramp.) *Color the ramp green.*

Day 1 picture

Day 2
SKILLS

Physical Science

- Represent observations of the physical world in a variety of ways
- Become familiar with a ramp (inclined plane—simple machine)
- Understand that ramps (simple machines) are used for a specific purpose

Literacy

Oral Language Development

- Use descriptive language

Comprehension

- Recall details
- Make connections using illustrations, prior knowledge, or real-life experiences

Reinforcing the Concept

Reread the Day 1 story. Then reinforce this week's science concept by guiding a discussion about the story. Say:

We learned that ramps make work easier. Why did Tiffany and Sara need a ramp? (to get the wagon full of blocks up the stairs)

Distribute the Day 2 activity and crayons. Then say:

Day 2 activity

- *Point to box 1. Is this person using a ramp to make work easier? Color the happy face for* **yes** *or the sad face for* **no**. (yes) *What work is this person doing?* (pushing a box up a ramp)

- *Point to box 2. Is this person using a ramp to make work easier? Color the happy face for* **yes** *or the sad face for* **no**. (no)

- *Point to box 3. Is this person using a ramp to make work easier? Color the happy face for* **yes** *or the sad face for* **no**. (yes) *What work is this boy doing?* (rolling himself up a ramp into a building)

- *Point to box 4. Is this person using a ramp to make work easier? Color the happy face for* **yes** *or the sad face for* **no**. (no)

Day 3
SKILLS

Physical Science

- Represent observations of the physical world in a variety of ways
- Become familiar with a ramp (inclined plane—simple machine)
- Understand that ramps (simple machines) are used for a specific purpose

Literacy

Oral Language Development

- Name and describe pictured objects

Comprehension

- Recall details
- Make connections using illustrations, prior knowledge, or real-life experiences

Identifying the Concept

To introduce the activity, guide a discussion that helps children recall the Day 1 story. Say:

Tiffany and Sara's dad made a ramp so they could pull the wagon up the stairs. How did he make the ramp? (He put a flat board over the stairs.)

Distribute the Day 3 activity and crayons. Say:

Day 3 activity

- *Look at the picture. Circle all of the people who are using a ramp to make their work easier. Put your crayon down when you are finished.*

Allow children time to complete the activity. After they are finished, say:

- *Let's talk about the pictures you circled. Raise your hand if you circled the man pushing the wheelbarrow with plants in it.* (children respond) *Why did you circle him?* (He is using a ramp to make it easier to push the wheelbarrow.)

- *Raise your hand if you circled the woman who is walking the dog.* (children respond) *Why* <u>*didn't*</u> *you circle her?* (She is not using a ramp to make work easier.)

Repeat the process with the remaining pictures.

Day 4
SKILLS

Physical Science

• Represent observations of the physical world in a variety of ways

• Become familiar with a ramp (inclined plane—simple machine)

• Understand that ramps (simple machines) are used for a specific purpose

Literacy

Oral Language Development

• Use descriptive language

Comprehension

• Make connections using illustrations, prior knowledge, or real-life experiences

Applying the Concept

Introduce the activity by saying:

People use ramps to make it easier to do things. Raise your hand if you've ever gone down a slide before. (children respond) *A slide is a type of ramp! A slide makes it easier and faster to get down to the ground.*

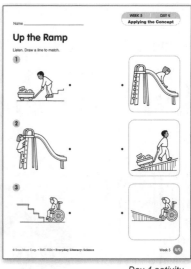

Day 4 activity

Distribute the Day 4 activity and crayons. Say:

• *Point to the first picture. What does it show?* (a boy standing at the bottom of the stairs with a wagon full of toys) *Would a ramp make it easier for the boy to pull his wagon up the stairs?* (yes) *Draw a line to the picture that shows a boy pulling a wagon up a ramp.*

• *Point to picture 2. What does it show?* (a girl going up the steps of a slide) *Remember, a slide is a ramp. A ramp makes it easier for the girl to get down to the ground. Draw a line to the picture that shows a girl sliding down a ramp.*

• *Point to picture 3. What does it show?* (a girl in a wheelchair at the bottom of the stairs) *Would a ramp make it easier for the girl to get up the stairs?* (yes) *Draw a line to the picture that shows the girl going up a ramp.*

Day 5
SKILLS

Physical Science

• Become familiar with a ramp (inclined plane—simple machine)

• Understand that ramps (simple machines) are used for a specific purpose

Scientific Thinking & Inquiry

• Gather information through the use of one or more of the senses

• Explore physical properties of objects and materials

• Experiment with simple machines

Home–School Connection p. 50
Spanish version available (see p. 2)

Hands-on Science Activity

Reinforce this week's science concept with the following hands-on activity:

Materials: large blocks or thick books; heavy cardboard or other sturdy, flat surface; and toy cars and other objects that can be rolled

Preparation: Use classroom blocks to build "stairs" in the area of the room in which the children will conduct the experiment.

Activity: Have children work together to build a ramp. First have them send a car down the stairs and then down the ramp to see which structure the car goes down (and up) more easily. Record the results. Allow children to continue building different-sized stairs and ramps.

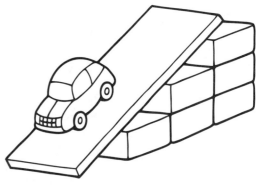

Up the Ramp

Name _____

Up the Ramp

Listen. Color the happy face for **yes**. Color the sad face for **no**.

Name _____

Up the Ramp

Circle the people who are using a ramp to make their work easier.

Everyday Literacy: Science • EMC 5024 • © Evan-Moor Corp.

Name _____

Up the Ramp

Listen. Draw a line to match.

Name _____

What I Learned

What to Do

Have your child look at the picture below and circle the people who are using a ramp to make their work easier. Then discuss how using a ramp makes the work easier.

WEEK 5

Home–School Connection

Science Concept: A ramp is easier to go up and down than stairs are.

To Parents

This week your child learned how ramps make work easier.

What to Do Next

Help your child build a simple ramp using items around your house such as blocks, books, or baking sheets. Then roll an item such as a toy car or a ball down the ramp. If you have stairs, you might try to roll the same item down the stairs and discuss which was easier, the ramp or the stairs.

WEEK 6

Concept

Living things have basic needs.

What Animals Need

Science Objective:
To help children understand that animals are living things that need water, food, and safe places

Science Vocabulary:
food, needs, place, safe, safety, water

Day 1 SKILLS

Life Science

- Represent observations of living things in a variety of ways
- Understand that people, animals, and plants are living things that have basic needs
- Identify food, water, and safe places

Literacy

Oral Language Development

- Respond orally to simple questions

Comprehension

- Recall details
- Make inferences and draw conclusions
- Make connections using illustrations, prior knowledge, or real-life experiences
- Listen to stories being read aloud

Introducing the Concept

Distribute the Day 1 activity page to each child. Have children look at the picture as they answer your questions. Say:

This backyard is a friendly place for animals. Animals need water to drink, food to eat, and safe places to stay.

- *Name the animals you see in this picture.* (birds, butterfly, lizard)
- *Some people have birdbaths in their backyards. The birdbaths hold clean water. Do you see water in the birdbath?* (yes)
- *Some people have bird feeders in their backyards. The bird feeders hold seeds for birds to eat. Do you see a bird at the bird feeder?* (yes)
- *A bird built a safe place in the tree. Do you see a safe place?* (yes)

Listening to the Story

Prepare children to listen to the story. Say: *Listen and look at the picture as I read a story about birds that live in a backyard.*

My backyard is a friendly place for birds. It has water, food, and safe places for them. Birds need water. I pour clean water into the birdbath. The birds come there to have a drink or take a bath. Birds also need food. My backyard has flowers, insects, and seeds that birds like to eat. Birds need safe places to live. A family of birds lives high up in the big tree. The baby birds are safe in their nest. Birds like my backyard!

Confirming Understanding

Distribute crayons or markers. Reinforce the science concept by asking children questions about the story. Ask:

- *Do birds need clean water to drink and take a bath?* (yes) *Make a blue dot on the bird that is in the birdbath.*
- *Do birds need food?* (yes) *Make a red dot on each bird that is eating.*
- *Do birds need safe places?* (yes) *Circle the birds that are in a safe place.*

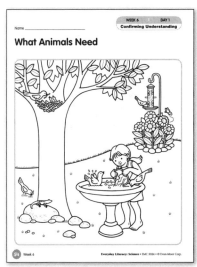

Day 1 picture

Life Science

• Represent observations of living things in a variety of ways

• Understand that people, animals, and plants are living things that have basic needs

• Identify food, water, and safe places

Literacy

Oral Language Development

• Respond orally to simple questions

Comprehension

• Recall details

• Make inferences and draw conclusions

Reinforcing the Concept

Reread the Day 1 story. Then reinforce this week's science concept by guiding a discussion about the story. Say:

Our story was about the things that animals need. Birds are animals. Why was the girl's backyard a good place for birds? (It had water, food, and safe places.)

Distribute the Day 2 activity and crayons. Allow children to color the happy or sad face each time before asking the next question. Say:

- *Listen carefully and follow my directions. Point to box 1. Animals need water. Did the girl put clean water in the birdbath? Color the happy face for **yes** or the sad face for **no**.* (yes)

- *Point to box 2. Animals need food. Is the bird eating seeds from the bird feeder? Color the happy face for **yes** or the sad face for **no**.* (yes) *Where else can the bird get food?* (from flowers and grass)

- *Look at box 3. Animals need safe places to hide. Is the lizard in a safe place? Color the happy face for **yes** or the sad face for **no**.* (no)

- *Look at box 4. Animals need safe places to raise their babies. The baby birds are in a nest. Are they in a safe place? Color the happy face for **yes** or the sad face for **no**.* (yes)

Day 2 activity

Life Science

• Represent observations of living things in a variety of ways

• Understand that people, animals, and plants are living things that have basic needs

• Identify food, water, and safe places

Literacy

Oral Language Development

• Respond orally to simple questions

Comprehension

• Make inferences and draw conclusions

Applying the Concept

Introduce the activity by saying:

Animals need food, water, and safe places. Yesterday we read about birds that live in a backyard. Can you name other animals you might see in a backyard? (answers vary)

Then distribute the Day 3 activity and crayons. Say:

- *Point to number 1. Put your finger on the bird. Where can the bird go to eat seeds?* (to the bird feeder) *Use a crayon to trace the line. Start at the bird and follow the line to the bird feeder.*

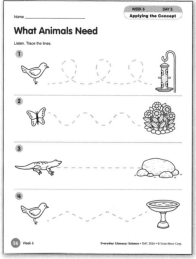

Day 3 activity

- *Point to number 2. Put your finger on the butterfly. Where can the butterfly go to find food?* (to the flowers) *Use a crayon to trace the line. Start at the butterfly and follow the line to the flowers.*

- *Point to number 3. Put your finger on the little lizard. Where can the lizard go to hide?* (under the rocks) *Use a crayon to trace the line. Start at the lizard and follow the line to the rocks.*

- *Point to number 4. Put your finger on the bird. Where can the bird go to drink?* (the birdbath) *Trace the line with a crayon.*

Day 4
SKILLS

Life Science

• Represent observations of living things in a variety of ways

• Understand that people, animals, and plants are living things that have basic needs

• Identify food, water, and safe places

Literacy

Oral Language Development

• Respond orally to simple questions

Comprehension

• Recall details

• Make inferences and draw conclusions

Applying the Concept

Introduce the activity by saying:

Animals find food, water, and safety in many different places. Some animals live in backyards. What animals live in your backyard? (answers vary)

Day 4 activity

Then distribute the Day 4 activity and crayons. Say:

• *Put your finger on row number 1. Point to each picture as I name it:* **flowers, bird feeder, cookie jar.** *Which ones hold food for backyard animals?* (flowers and bird feeder) *Circle the flowers and the bird feeder.*

• *Put your finger on row number 2. Point to each picture as I name it:* **water bottle, birdbath, rain puddle.** *Which ones hold water for animals?* (birdbath and rain puddle) *Circle the birdbath and the rain puddle.*

• *Put your finger on row number 3. Point to each picture as I name it:* **rock pile, car, tree.** *Which ones are safe places for animals to live or hide?* (rock pile and tree) *Circle the rock pile and the tree.*

• *Put your finger on row number 4. Point to each picture as I name it:* **elephant, butterfly, bird.** *Which ones are backyard animals?* (butterfly and bird) *Circle the butterfly and the bird.*

Day 5
SKILLS

Life Science

• Represent observations of living things in a variety of ways

• Understand that people, animals, and plants are living things that have basic needs

• Identify food, water, and safe places

Scientific Thinking & Inquiry

• Gather and record information through simple observations and investigations

---

Home–School Connection p. 58
Spanish version available (see p. 2)

Hands-on Science Activity

Reinforce this week's science concept with the following hands-on activity:

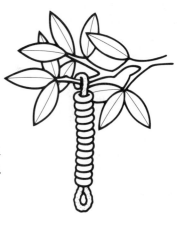

Materials: unsweetened cereal rings such as Cheerios®, one or more pipe cleaners and one paper plate or plastic tray per child

Preparation: Place cereal on a paper plate for each child. Make a loop on one end of each pipe cleaner.

Activity: Introduce the activity by saying:

Birds live in many places. They find food in many places. Let's make a bird feeder and hang it in a tree. Then birds will eat the food from it.

Then demonstrate how to string the cereal onto a pipe cleaner. Make sure the loop is at the bottom of the pipe cleaner. When the cereal is almost to the top of the pipe cleaner, bend the tip to make a hook. Then take the children outside and help them hang their bird feeders in a tree or bush that is visible from the classroom. Have children keep an eye out for feeding birds!

Note: It will take some children longer than others to make a feeder, so provide extra materials for those who finish and want to make more feeders.

Name _____

What Animals Need

Everyday Literacy: Science • EMC 5024 • © Evan-Moor Corp.

Name _____

What Animals Need

Listen. Color the happy face for **yes**. Color the sad face for **no**.

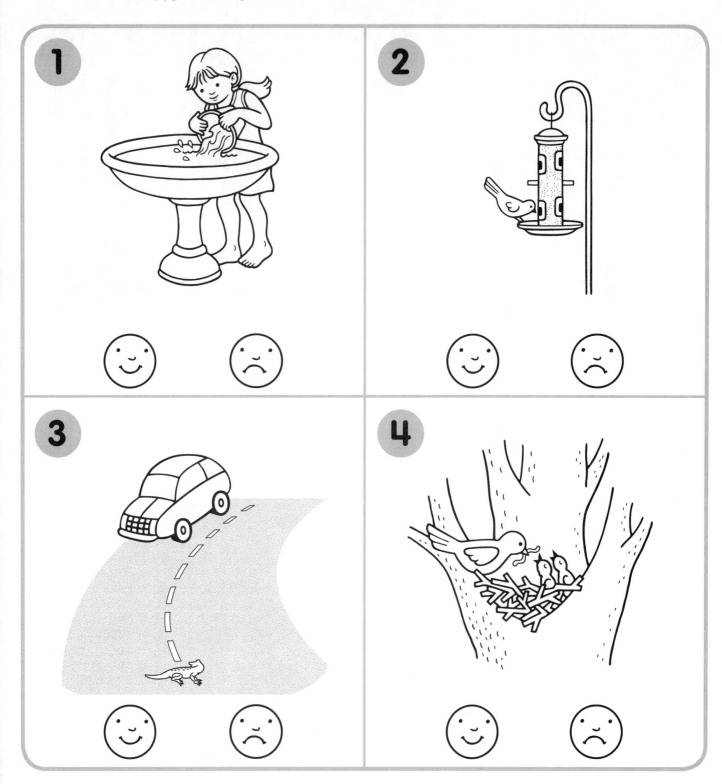

Name _____

What Animals Need

Listen. Trace the lines.

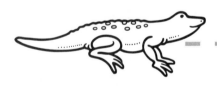 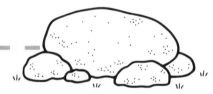

Everyday Literacy: Science • EMC 5024 • © Evan-Moor Corp.

Name _____

What Animals Need

Listen. Circle the correct pictures.

  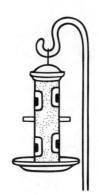 

  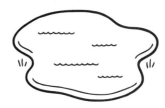

Name _____

What I Learned

What to Do
Have your child look at the picture below. Ask him or her to point to all of the animals in the picture. Then have your child tell you what those animals drink, what they eat, and where they find safe places in the backyard. Then have your child color the picture.

Science Concept: Living things have basic needs.

To Parents
This week your child learned that animals need water to drink, food to eat, and safe places to stay.

What to Do Next
Go on a discovery walk with your child. Look for animals, their homes, and the foods they eat.

Everyday Literacy: Science • EMC 5024 • © Evan-Moor Corp.

What People Need

Science Objective:
To help children understand that people are living things who need air, water, food, and sleep

Science Vocabulary:
air, breathe, food, living things, needs, sleep, water

Day 1
SKILLS

Life Science
- Represent observations of living things in a variety of ways
- Understand that people, animals, and plants are living things that have basic needs

Literacy

Oral Language Development
- Respond orally to simple questions

Comprehension
- Recall details
- Make connections using illustrations, prior knowledge, or real-life experiences
- Listen to stories being read aloud
- Make inferences and draw conclusions

Introducing the Concept

Distribute the Day 1 activity page to each child and point to the pictures in the circle as you discuss each of the four needs. Say:

People are living things. People need to breathe air, drink water, eat food, and sleep. What food do you eat? (answers vary) *Point to the picture of the girl eating.*

- *Do you drink water?* (yes) *Point to the picture of the girl drinking.*
- *Do you sleep at night?* (yes) *Point to the picture of the girl sleeping.*

Listening to the Story

Prepare children to listen to the story. Say: *Listen and look at the picture as I read a story about a girl who learns about the things that people need.*

At bedtime, Alisa's mom reads her a book about what people need. Alisa learns that people need air to breathe. She thinks about how she and her mom go to the park to get fresh air. Next, she learns that people need water. Alisa thinks about how she drinks water from the water fountain when she's playing at the park. She also learns that people need food. Alisa thinks about all the yummy food her mom makes. Alisa yawns as her mom reads the last page of the book. It says that people need sleep, too. Alisa's glad about that because she's tired and ready to go to sleep!

Confirming Understanding

Distribute crayons or markers. Reinforce the science concept by asking children questions about the story. Ask:

- *What do people breathe?* (air) *Air is everywhere, but we cannot see it.*
- *What do people need to drink?* (water) *Make a blue dot on the water fountain.*
- *What do people need to eat?* (food) *Make a red dot on the food Alisa is eating.*
- *What do people need when they are tired?* (sleep) *Make a purple dot on Alisa's blanket.*

Day 1 picture

Day 2
SKILLS

Life Science

- Represent observations of living things in a variety of ways

- Understand that people, animals, and plants are living things that have basic needs

Literacy

Oral Language Development

- Respond orally to simple questions

Comprehension

- Recall details

- Make inferences and draw conclusions

Reinforcing the Concept

Reread the Day 1 story. Then reinforce this week's science concept by guiding a discussion about the story. Say:

Our story was about things that people need. What do people need? (air, water, food, sleep)

Distribute the Day 2 activity and crayons. Allow children to color the happy or sad face each time before asking the next question. Say:

- *Point to box 1. Air is everywhere, but we cannot see it. Alisa is playing outside in the fresh air. Do people need to breathe air? Color the happy face for **yes** or the sad face for **no**.* (yes)

- *Point to box 2. Alisa is watching TV. Do people need to watch TV? Color the happy face for **yes** or the sad face for **no**.* (no)

- *Point to box 3. Alisa is drinking water. Do people need to drink water? Color the happy face for **yes** or the sad face for **no**.* (yes)

- *Look at box 4. Alisa is asleep in her bed. Do people need to sleep? Color the happy face for **yes** or the sad face for **no**.* (yes)

Day 2 activity

Day 3
SKILLS

Life Science

- Represent observations of living things in a variety of ways

- Understand that people, animals, and plants are living things that have basic needs

Literacy

Oral Language Development

- Respond orally to simple questions

Comprehension

- Make connections using illustrations, prior knowledge, or real-life experiences

Identifying the Concept

Distribute the Day 3 activity and crayons. Then introduce the activity by saying:

Tom wants to be healthy and strong. Let's help Tom find everything he needs.

- *Tom needs to eat food. Point to the picture of food. What kind of food is it?* (banana) *Use a yellow crayon to circle the banana.*

- *Tom needs to drink water. Point to the picture that shows water. What is it?* (a drinking fountain) *Use a blue crayon to circle the drinking fountain.*

- *Tom needs to get enough sleep. Point to the picture that shows somewhere Tom can sleep. What is it?* (a bed) *Use a red crayon to circle the bed.*

- *Tom needs to breathe air. We cannot see it, but air is everywhere. Tom breathes with his nose. Point to the picture of Tom's nose. Use a brown crayon to circle the nose.*

Day 3 activity

Life Science

• Represent observations of living things in a variety of ways

• Understand that people, animals, and plants are living things that have basic needs

Literacy

Oral Language Development

• Respond orally to simple questions

Comprehension

• Make inferences and draw conclusions

• Make connections using illustrations, prior knowledge, or real-life experiences

Applying the Concept

Distribute the Day 4 activity and crayons. Then guide children through the activity by saying:

• *Picture 1 shows a boy eating food. People need food. Do you see any other pictures of food? (yes) What kind of food is it? (an apple; fruit) Draw a line from the picture of the boy eating to the apple.*

• *Picture 2 shows a girl drinking water. People need water. What other picture shows water? (water bottle) Draw a line from the picture of the girl drinking to the water bottle.*

Day 4 activity

• *Picture 3 shows a boy sleeping. People need sleep. What other picture shows someone sleeping? (baby in basket) Draw a line from the picture of the boy sleeping to the sleeping baby.*

• *Picture 4 shows a boy running outside. People need fresh air and exercise. What other picture shows someone breathing fresh air? (boy leaning out window) Draw a line from the picture of the boy running to the boy breathing fresh air.*

Life Science

• Represent observations of living things in a variety of ways

• Understand that people, animals, and plants are living things that have basic needs

Scientific Thinking & Inquiry

• Gather information through the use of one or more of the senses

• Gather and record information through simple observations and investigations

Home–School Connection p. 66
Spanish version available (see p. 2)

Hands-on Science Activity

Reinforce this week's science concept with the following hands-on activity:

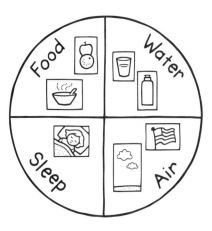

Materials: clip art or magazine images that show food, water, outdoor scenes, and people sleeping; bulletin board paper, glue sticks

Preparation: Gather enough pictures to distribute at least one picture per child. Draw a large circle on bulletin board paper. Divide the circle into four sections labeled **Food, Water, Sleep,** and **Air.** Glue a picture beside each label to represent it. (Pictures to represent **air** might show the sky, a flag blowing in the wind, etc.)

Activity: Display the chart. Then distribute at least one picture to each child. Point to the chart and say:

• *You know that people need certain things to live. Let's name those things on the chart:* **Food, Water, Sleep, Air.**

• *The first section of the chart says* **Food.** *Who has a picture that shows food?*

Have one child at a time name his or her picture and glue it in the **Food** section. Then ask for pictures that go in each of the other sections. (When discussing pictures of air, point out that air is everywhere. We cannot see it, but we can sometimes see what it does. For example, it blows the leaves on the trees.) Hang the chart where children can reach it to point to and discuss their pictures during independent time.

Name _____

What People Need

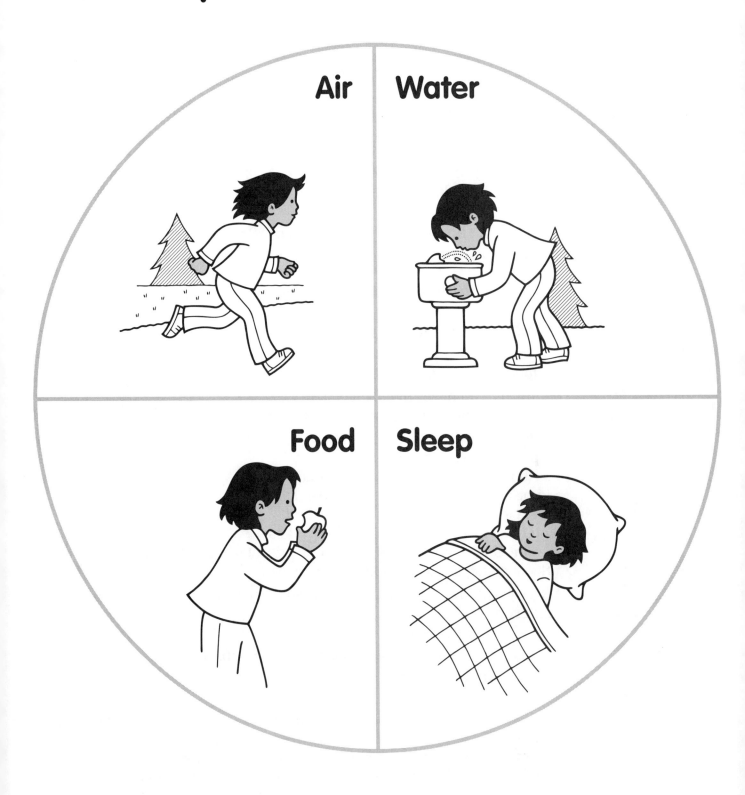

Air   Water

Food   Sleep

Name _____

What People Need

Listen. Color the happy face for **yes**. Color the sad face for **no**.

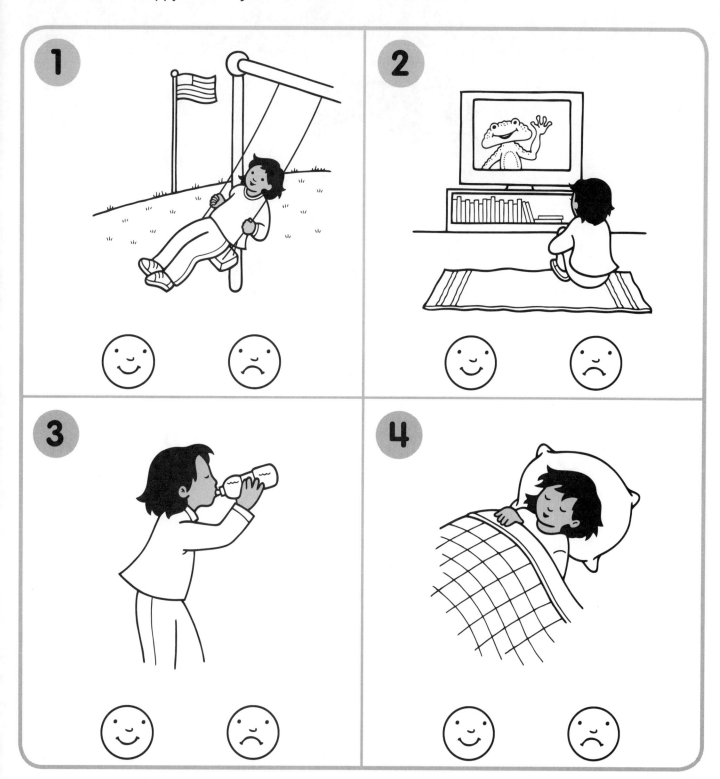

Name _____

What People Need

Listen. Circle the things that people need.

Name _____

What People Need

Listen. Draw lines to match.

1

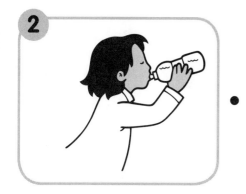

2

3

4

Name _____

What I Learned

What to Do
Have your child look at the pictures below. Ask him or her to point to each of these things that people need: air, water, food, sleep. Then have your child color the pictures.

Science Concept: Living things have basic needs.

To Parents
This week your child learned that people need air, water, food, and sleep.

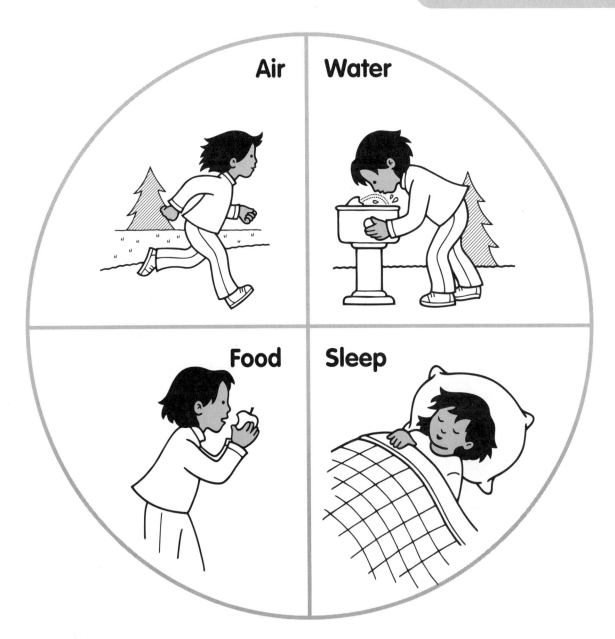

Air   Water

Food   Sleep

What to Do Next
Discuss your family's daily routine. Point out when and how your child's basic needs are being met. For example, say: *You need water and food to be healthy. That is why you take a water bottle and healthful foods for lunch to school with you every day.*

What Plants Need

Science Objective:
To help children understand that plants are living things that need soil, water, and sunlight

Science Vocabulary:
dirt, grow, light, plant, soil, sunlight, tomato, water

Day 1
SKILLS

Life Science
- Represent observations of living things in a variety of ways
- Understand that people, animals, and plants are living things that have basic needs

Literacy

Oral Language Development
- Respond orally to simple questions

Comprehension
- Recall details
- Make connections using illustrations, prior knowledge, or real-life experiences
- Listen to stories being read aloud
- Make inferences and draw conclusions

Introducing the Concept

Distribute the Day 1 activity page to each child. Point to the indoor and outdoor plants, the soil, the hose, the watering can, and the sun as you refer to them. Say:

- *Plants are living things. Plants need soil, water, and sunlight.*
- *Plants can grow indoors in pots of soil. They can also grow outside in the ground. Another name for soil is **dirt**.*
- *Plants need water. Plants that are outside get water when it rains. They also get water when a person uses a hose to water them. People also water plants that are indoors.*
- *Plants need sunlight. Plants get sunlight from the sun. The sun shines on plants during the day.*

Listening to the Story

Prepare children to listen to the story. Say: *Listen and look at the picture as I read a story about children who are growing plants.*

My friends and I grew tomato plants at school. We learned that plants need soil, water, and sunlight to grow, so we knew just what to do. First, we put soil into pots. Then we put little plants into the soil. We put some of the plants indoors and some outside. The rain watered the plants that were outside. I used a watering can to water the plants that were indoors. Next, we made sure the plants got lots of sunshine. The plants grew bigger. Soon there were green tomatoes next to the leaves! My friends and I like growing plants.

Confirming Understanding

Distribute crayons or markers. Reinforce the science concept by asking these questions:

- *Do plants need soil? (yes) Another word for soil is **dirt**. Make a brown dot on some soil.*
- *Do plants need water? (yes) Make a blue dot on a raindrop.*
- *Do plants need sunlight? (yes) Draw a yellow sun in the sky.*
- *Can plants grow indoors and outside? (yes) Make a green dot on an indoor plant and an outdoor plant.*

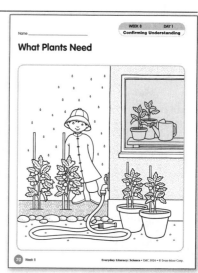

Day 1 picture

Life Science

• Represent observations of living things in a variety of ways

• Understand that people, animals, and plants are living things that have basic needs

Literacy

Oral Language Development

• Respond orally to simple questions

Comprehension

• Recall details

• Make inferences and draw conclusions

Reinforcing the Concept

Reread the Day 1 story. Then reinforce this week's science concept by guiding a discussion about the story. Say:

Our story told us about what plants need. Ask:

• *What do plants need?* (soil, water, sunlight)

Distribute the Day 2 activity and crayons. Say:

• *Point to box 1. Plants need water. Is this plant getting water? Color the happy face for **yes** or the sad face for **no**.* (yes)

• *Point to box 2. Plants need sunlight. Is this plant getting sunlight? Color the happy face for **yes** or the sad face for **no**.* (yes)

• *Point to box 3. Plants need soil. Is this plant in soil? Color the happy face for **yes** or the sad face for **no**.* (no)

• *Point to box 4. Plants can grow outside and indoors. Are these plants growing outside? Color the happy face for **yes** or the sad face for **no**.* (yes)

Day 2 activity

Life Science

• Represent observations of living things in a variety of ways

• Understand that people, animals, and plants are living things that have basic needs

Literacy

Oral Language Development

• Respond orally to simple questions

Comprehension

• Make inferences and draw conclusions

Applying the Concept

Distribute the Day 3 activity and crayons. Then introduce the activity by saying:

The children in our story learned that plants need soil, water, and sunlight. The boy in this picture is growing a plant, too. Let's help him.

• *A tomato plant needs a big pot to grow in. What goes into the pot first with the plant?* (soil) *Put your finger on the picture of the boy putting soil into the pot. Draw a line from that picture to the number 1.*

• *What does the boy do next after the soil and the plant are in the pot?* (He gives it water.) *Put your finger on the picture of the boy watering the plant. Draw a line from that picture to the number 2.*

• *What happens to the plant after it has soil, water, and sunshine?* (It grows bigger; It grows tomatoes.) *Put your finger on the picture of the big plant with tomatoes on it. Draw a line from that picture to the number 3.*

Day 3 activity

Life Science

• Represent observations of living things in a variety of ways

• Understand that people, animals, and plants are living things that have basic needs

Literacy

Comprehension

• Make inferences and draw conclusions

Extending the Concept

Distribute the Day 4 activity and crayons. Then introduce the activity by saying:

All plants need soil, water, and sunlight. There are many different kinds of plants. Flowers are plants, trees are plants, bushes are plants, and grass is a plant, too.

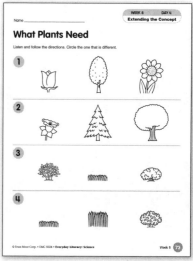

- *Point to row 1. Flowers are plants. Look at all of the pictures in this row. Circle the picture that is <u>not</u> a flower.*

- *Point to row 2. Trees are plants. Look at all of the pictures in this row. Circle the picture that is <u>not</u> a tree.*

- *Point to row 3. Bushes are plants. Look at all of the pictures in this row. Circle the picture that is <u>not</u> a bush.*

- *Point to row 4. Grass is a plant. Look at all of the pictures in this row. Circle the picture that is <u>not</u> grass.*

Day 4 activity

Life Science

• Represent observations of living things in a variety of ways

• Understand that people, animals, and plants are living things that have basic needs

• Explore characteristics of living things

Scientific Thinking & Inquiry

• Gather and record information through simple observations and investigations

Home–School Connection p. 74
Spanish version available (see p. 2)

Hands-on Activity

Reinforce this week's science concept as children apply processes of scientific inquiry—observing, describing, and recording.

Materials: two small green plants, a brown paper bag

Activity: Place the two plants in a sunny window, covering one with a paper bag. Say:

You know that plants need soil, water, and sunlight. What do you think will happen if I cover one plant? Will it get the sunlight it needs? What will happen to that plant?

Over the next few weeks, water both plants as needed, but always keep the one plant covered. Every few days, allow the children to examine the plants and describe what they see. End the investigation by displaying the unhealthy plant and asking:

What happened to this plant? Why does it look so bad?
(It didn't get any sunlight; Plants need light to grow.)

Have children draw a picture of the healthy and unhealthy plants.

Name _____

What Plants Need

Name _____

What Plants Need

Listen. Color the happy face for **yes**. Color the sad face for **no**.

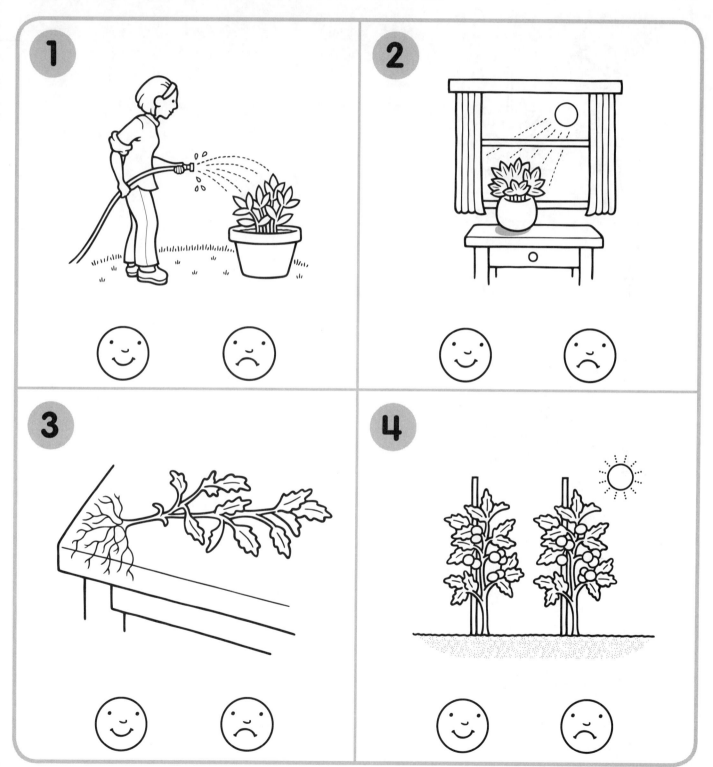

Name _____

What Plants Need

Listen. Then draw a line from the picture to **1**, **2**, or **3** to show what happened first, second, and third.

• •   1

• • 2

• • 3

Everyday Literacy: Science • EMC 5024 • © Evan-Moor Corp.

Name _____

What Plants Need

Listen and follow the directions. Circle the one that is different.

 1

2

3

4

Name _____

What I Learned

What to Do
Have your child look at the picture below. Ask him or her to point to the things a plant needs in order to grow (soil, water, sunlight). Ask your child which of these things is missing from the picture (sunlight). Then have your child draw a sun in the picture and color the picture.

WEEK 8
Home–School Connection

Science Concept: Living things have basic needs.

To Parents
This week your child listened to a story about a boy's preschool class that grows tomatoes in large pots.

What to Do Next
Walk with your child outdoors to find plants growing. Ask your child: *How do these plants get water?* (rain, sprinklers, hose, etc.) *How do they get light?* (sun)

Everyday Literacy: Science • EMC 5024 • © Evan-Moor Corp.

WEEK 9

Concept
People have body parts.

Our Bodies Have Parts

Science Objective:
To help children understand that some of their body parts help them learn about the world around them

Science Vocabulary:
ears, eyes, feel, hands, hear, mouth, nose, see, senses, smell, taste, touch

---

Day 1
SKILLS

Life Science
• Represent observations of living things in a variety of ways
• Understand that people, animals, and plants are living things that have basic needs

Literacy

Oral Language Development
• Respond orally to simple questions

Comprehension
• Recall details
• Make connections using illustrations, prior knowledge, or real-life experiences
• Listen to stories being read aloud
• Make inferences and draw conclusions

Introducing the Concept

Introduce children to the concept that our body parts help us learn about the world. Point to each body part as you say:

• *We use our eyes to see, our ears to hear, our nose to smell, our mouth to taste, and our hands to feel or touch.*

• *Point to your eyes. Say, "I use my eyes to see." (children repeat) Point to your ears. Say, "I use my ears to hear." (children repeat)*

Continue the process for nose, mouth, and hands.

Listening to the Story

Distribute the Day 1 activity page and crayons. Say: *Listen and look at the picture as I read you a story about a girl who visits a petting zoo.*

I have body parts that tell me about the world around me. Today I went to the petting zoo at the Old Red Barn. I smelled the animals with my nose. I heard a goat say "maa-maa" with my ears. I looked at its big teeth with my eyes. I felt the goat's long brown hair with my hand. After I visited the petting zoo, I was ready to eat my peanut butter and jelly sandwich for lunch. I put it in my mouth and tasted it. I said, "Yum!"

Confirming Understanding

Distribute crayons. Develop the science concept by asking questions about the story. Ask:

• *What body part did the girl use to smell the animals?* (nose) *Circle her nose with red.*

• *What body part did she use to see the goat's teeth?* (eyes) *Color the girl's eyes.*

• *What body part did the girl use to hear the goat?* (ears) *Circle the girl's ear with blue.*

• *What did she use to feel the goat's hair?* (hands) *Circle the girl's hand with orange.*

• *What body part did the girl use to taste her sandwich?* (mouth) *Color the girl's mouth pink.*

Day 1 picture

Life Science

• Represent observations of living things in a variety of ways

• Understand that people, animals, and plants are living things that have basic needs

Literacy

Oral Language Development

• Respond orally to simple questions

Reinforcing the Concept

Reread the Day 1 story. Then reinforce this week's science concept by guiding a discussion about the story. Say:

Our story was about our body parts. What body part helps you see? (eyes) *smell?* (nose) *taste?* (mouth) *touch?* (hands) *hear?* (ears)

Distribute the Day 2 activity and crayons. Say:

• *Put your finger on the barn. What body part would you use to see the barn?* (eyes) *Make a circle around the eyes.*

• *Put your finger on the hay. What body part would you use to feel the hay?* (hand) *Make a circle around the hand.*

• *Put your finger on the apple. What body part would you use to taste the apple?* (mouth) *Make a circle around the mouth.*

• *Put your finger on the flower. What body part would you use to smell the flower?* (nose) *Make a circle around the nose.*

• *Put your finger on the goat. What body part would you use to hear it say "maa-maa"?* (ears) *Make a circle around the ear.*

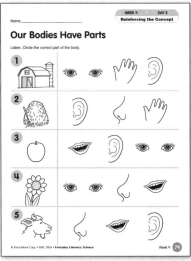

Day 2 activity

Life Science

• Represent observations of living things in a variety of ways

• Understand that people, animals, and plants are living things that have basic needs

Literacy

Oral Language Development

• Respond orally to simple questions

Comprehension

• Recall details

• Make inferences and draw conclusions

Developing the Concept

To introduce the activity, guide a discussion that helps children recall the Day 1 story. Say:

Our story was about parts of the body that we use to see, hear, smell, taste, and touch. Let's name the body parts: eyes, ears, nose, mouth, and hands.

Distribute the Day 3 activity and crayons. Say:

• *Listen and follow my directions. The boy tasted a sweet apple. What body part did he use to taste the apple?* (mouth) *Draw a line from the boy's mouth to the apple.*

• *The boy heard a bell ringing. What body part did he use to hear the bell?* (ears) *Draw a line from one of the boy's ears to the bell.*

• *The boy smelled animals in the barn. What body part did he use to smell?* (nose) *Draw a line from the boy's nose to the barn.*

• *The boy saw a little mouse run across the floor. What body part did he use to see?* (eyes) *Draw a line from one of the boy's eyes to the mouse.*

• *The boy felt the cat's soft fur. What body part did he use to feel the fur?* (hands) *Draw a line from one of the boy's hands to the cat.*

Day 3 activity

Life Science

• Represent observations of living things in a variety of ways

• Understand that people, animals, and plants are living things that have basic needs

Literacy

Oral Language Development

• Respond orally to simple questions

Comprehension

• Make inferences and draw conclusions

Applying the Concept

Introduce the activity by saying:

We use some of our body parts to learn about the world. What can our body parts tell us about an apple? (e.g., Our eyes can tell us what it looks like; Our mouth can tell us what it tastes like; etc.)

Day 4 activity

Distribute the Day 4 activity and crayons. Say:

• *Listen to this story: A boy named Justin was walking outdoors. He saw an apple tree full of red apples. What body part did he use to see?* (eyes) *Draw a line from his eye to the apple tree.*

• *Justin pulled an apple off a low branch. It was smooth. What body part did he use to touch the apple?* (hand) *Draw a line from his hand to an apple on the tree.*

• *When Justin bit into the apple, it tasted sweet. What body part did he use to taste the apple?* (mouth) *Draw a line from his mouth to the apple that has a bite in it.*

• *Plop! Justin heard an apple fall from the tree. What body part did he use to hear it?* (ears) *Draw a line from his ear to the apple that fell from the tree.*

Life Science

• Represent observations of living things in a variety of ways

• Understand that people, animals, and plants are living things that have basic needs

• Explore characteristics of living things

Scientific Thinking & Inquiry

• Gather information through the use of one or more of the senses

Home–School Connection p. 82
Spanish version available (see p. 2)

Hands-on Science Activity

Reinforce this week's science concept with the following hands-on activity:

Materials: individual pictures of an ear, a hand, a nose, and a mouth; a variety of items that children can hear, touch, smell, and taste, such as bells, blocks, beanbags; scraps of velvet and wool, cotton balls, sandpaper, aluminum foil, smooth and bumpy rocks; cinnamon sticks, perfumes, chocolate, flowers; fruit, crackers, popcorn, jelly beans, celery (Avoid peanuts or other common food-allergy items.)

Preparation: Use the materials above to set up a **hear** center, a **touch** center, a **smell** center, and a **taste** center. Place the corresponding body part picture at each center.

Activity: Introduce the activity by saying:

We are going to use our body parts to learn more about the things on this table. We will use our ears to hear things and then we will talk about how they sound. We will use our hands to touch things and then talk about how they feel. We will use our nose to smell things and then talk about how they smell. We will use our mouths to eat things and then talk about how they taste.

Encourage discussion as children visit each center. Model using descriptive words such as *smooth, rough, sweet, salty*, etc.

Our Bodies Have Parts

Name _____

Our Bodies Have Parts

Listen. Circle the correct part of the body.

1

2

3

4

5

Name _____

Our Bodies Have Parts

Listen and follow the directions.

Name _____

Our Bodies Have Parts

Listen to the story. Draw lines to show the four senses the boy uses.

Name _____

What I Learned

What to Do
Have your child look at the picture. Ask him or her to point to each body part and tell what the girl used it for: eyes (see the goat's teeth); ears (hear goat say "maa-maa"); nose (smell the animals); hand (pet goat's hair); mouth (taste her peanut butter and jelly sandwich). Then have your child color the picture.

Science Concept: People have body parts.

To Parents
This week your child learned that we use parts of our body to sense the world around us.

What to Do Next
Have your child play a game of "What Do Your Eyes See?" Place three small items on a tray. Give your child several seconds to study what is on the tray. Then have your child close his or her eyes while you remove one item. When he or she opens them, have your child tell you what is missing.

WEEK **10**

Concept
Plants have parts.

Plants Have Parts

Science Objective:
To help children understand that trees are plants and that plants have parts that help them live and grow

Science Vocabulary:
ground, grow, leaves, live, plant, roots, shade, tree, trunk, water

Day 1 SKILLS

Life Science
• Represent observations of living things in a variety of ways
• Understand that people, animals, and plants are living things that have basic needs

Literacy

Oral Language Development
• Respond orally to simple questions

Comprehension
• Recall details
• Make connections using illustrations, prior knowledge, or real-life experiences
• Listen to stories being read aloud
• Make inferences and draw conclusions

Introducing the Concept

Distribute the Day 1 activity page. Then point to each part of the tree as you name it. Say:

• *A tree is a plant. Plants have parts. Roots are part of a tree. They are at the bottom of a tree under the ground. Have you ever seen tree roots?* (children respond)

• *A trunk is part of a tree. Have you ever touched a tree trunk? What did it feel like?* (children respond)

• *A leaf is part of a tree. Have you ever seen a leaf? What color was it?* (children respond)

Listening to the Story

Redirect children's attention to the Day 1 page. Say: *Listen and look at the picture as I read you a story about a boy who has his very own tree.*

Brian's grandpa likes plants. He has a big plant in his backyard. It is a tree. Brian's grandpa taught him that plants have parts that help them live and grow. Brian learned that a tree has roots that hold it in the ground. He learned that the roots soak up water from the ground. Brian also learned that a tree has a trunk that makes it stand tall. He learned that the trunk carries water up to the leaves. Brian's grandpa told him that the leaves make food for the tree. Now that Brian knows so much about plants, he likes them as much as his grandpa does!

Confirming Understanding

Distribute crayons or markers. Reinforce the science concept by asking children questions about the story. Ask:

• *What is in Brian's grandpa's backyard?* (a tree) *Is a tree a plant?* (yes) *Do plants have parts?* (yes)

• *What part of the tree holds it in the ground?* (the roots) *Circle the tree's roots.*

• *What part of the tree makes it stand up?* (the trunk) *Color the trunk brown.*

• *What part of the tree makes food?* (leaves) *Color some of the leaves green.*

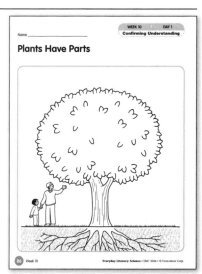

Day 1 picture

Life Science
- Represent observations of living things in a variety of ways
- Understand that people, animals, and plants are living things that have basic needs

Literacy

Oral Language Development
- Respond orally to simple questions

Comprehension
- Recall details
- Make connections using illustrations, prior knowledge, or real-life experiences
- Listen to stories being read aloud
- Make inferences and draw conclusions

Reinforcing the Concept

Reread the Day 1 story. Then reinforce this week's science concept by guiding a discussion about the story. Say:

Our story was about the parts of a tree. What parts does a tree have? (roots, trunk, leaves)

Distribute the Day 2 activity and crayons. Say:

- *Point to box 1. Roots hold the tree in the ground. Does this tree have roots? Color the happy face for **yes** or the sad face for **no**.* (yes) *Point to the roots.*

- *Now point to box 2. The trunk helps the tree stand up. Does this tree have a trunk? Color the happy face for **yes** or the sad face for **no**.* (yes) *Point to the trunk.*

- *Now point to box 3. The leaves make food for the tree. Does this tree have leaves on it? Color the happy face for **yes** or the sad face for **no**.* (yes) *Point to the leaves.*

- *Point to box 4. Does this tree have all its parts? Color the happy face for **yes** or the sad face for **no**.* (no) *What part is missing?* (leaves) *Where are they?* (on the ground)

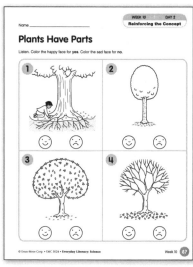

Day 2 activity

Life Science
- Represent observations of living things in a variety of ways
- Understand that people, animals, and plants are living things that have basic needs

Literacy

Oral Language Development
- Respond orally to simple questions

Comprehension
- Make connections using illustrations, prior knowledge, or real-life experiences
- Make inferences and draw conclusions

Identifying the Concept

To introduce the activity, guide a discussion that helps children recall the Day 1 story. Say:

In our story, Brian's grandpa taught him that plants have parts that help them live and grow. What do plants need? (water, soil, sun)

Then distribute the Day 3 activity and crayons and say:

- *Look at the big picture of a tree. Let's name the parts together. Point to each one, starting at the top: leaves, trunk, roots.*

- *Now look at the little pictures. What does picture 1 show?* (roots) *The roots soak up water for the tree. They hold the tree in the ground. Where are the roots?* (at the bottom) *Draw a line from picture 1 to the roots in the big picture.*

- *Look at picture 2. What does it show?* (leaves) *Leaves make food for the tree. They give people shade, too. Where are the leaves?* (at the top) *Draw a line from picture 2 to the leaves in the big picture.*

- *Look at picture 3. What does it show?* (a trunk) *The trunk makes the tree stand up. It also carries water up to the leaves. Where is the trunk?* (in the middle) *Draw a line from picture 3 to the trunk in the big picture.*

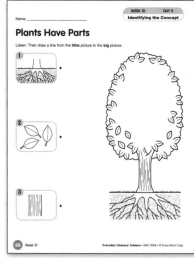

Day 3 activity

Life Science

• Represent observations of living things in a variety of ways

• Understand that people, animals, and plants are living things that have basic needs

Literacy

Oral Language Development

• Respond orally to simple questions

Comprehension

• Make connections using illustrations, prior knowledge, or real-life experiences

• Make inferences and draw conclusions

Applying the Concept

Introduce the activity by saying:

A tree has parts that do different jobs. Leaves make food for the tree. Have you ever touched a leaf? How did it feel? (flat, smooth, fuzzy, etc.) Leaves can look or feel different, but they all have the same job—to make food for a tree.

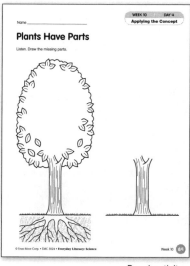

Day 4 activity

Distribute the Day 4 activity and crayons. Say:

• *Point to the tree. What are its parts? (leaves, trunk, roots)*

• *Point to the picture next to the tree. It is a tree, too. What parts are missing? (roots and leaves)*

• *First, use a green crayon to draw the missing leaves of the tree. Then put your crayon down.*

• *Next, use a brown crayon to draw the missing roots of the tree.*

• *When you are done, color the trunk of the tree brown.*

Life Science

• Represent observations of living things in a variety of ways

• Understand that people, animals, and plants are living things that have basic needs

• Explore characteristics of living things

Scientific Thinking & Inquiry

• Gather and record information through simple observations and investigations

Home–School Connection p. 90
Spanish version available (see p. 2)

Hands-on Science Activity

Reinforce this week's science concept with the following hands-on activity:

Materials: tree parts such as leaves, pieces of bark, small twigs, seeds or nuts; glue, one sheet of construction paper and one lunch bag per child

Preparation: Write each child's name on a paper bag and a sheet of construction paper.

Activity: Distribute the paper bags to children. Explain that they will take a discovery walk around the school and collect tree parts. Tell them that they will use the tree parts they collect to make a *collage,* or a picture.

• Take children outside to look for leaves, bark, and other tree parts. Have children place what they collect in their paper bags.

• After you return to the classroom, distribute the labeled construction paper to each child.

• Have children glue their tree parts on the construction paper to make a collage.

• Have children take turns telling the class about their tree-parts collage.

Plants Have Parts

Name _____

Plants Have Parts

Listen. Color the happy face for **yes**. Color the sad face for **no**.

Name _____

Plants Have Parts

Listen. Then draw a line from the **little** picture to the **big** picture.

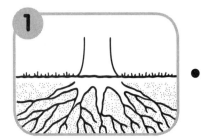

1

2

3

Name _____

Plants Have Parts

Listen. Draw the missing parts.

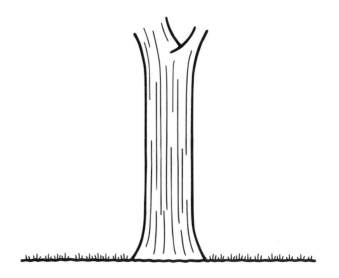

Name _____

What I Learned

What to Do
Have your child look at the picture below and point to the roots, trunk, and leaves. Then discuss the job each part does: The roots hold the tree in the ground and take in water. The trunk makes the tree stand up and carries water to the leaves. The leaves make food for the tree and give us shade.

Science Concept: Plants have parts.

To Parents
This week your child learned that a tree has roots, a trunk, and leaves and what each part does for the tree.

What to Do Next
Take a discovery walk with your child. Look at different plants and study their parts. Help your child notice things that are the same and different about the plants you see.

Everyday Literacy: Science • EMC 5024 • © Evan-Moor Corp.

Concept

Animals have body parts.

Animals Have Parts

Science Objective:
To help children understand that animals have body parts that help them do things

Science Vocabulary:
ears, fins, fur, legs, nose, paws, tail, trunk, whiskers, wings

Day 1
SKILLS

Life Science

• Represent observations of living things in a variety of ways

• Understand that people, animals, and plants are living things that have basic needs

Literacy

Oral Language Development

• Respond orally to simple questions

Comprehension

• Recall details

• Make connections using illustrations, prior knowledge, or real-life experiences

• Listen to stories being read aloud

• Make inferences and draw conclusions

Introducing the Concept

Distribute the Day 1 activity page. Then point to the cat's body parts as you talk about each one. Say:

• *Look at this cat. It has a nose. Its nose helps it smell. Point to the cat's nose. Name other animals that have a nose.* (children respond)

• *A cat has ears. Point to the cat's ears. Its ears help it hear. Name other animals that have ears.* (children respond)

• *A cat has four legs that help it walk. Point to one of the cat's legs. Name other animals that have legs.* (children respond)

• *A cat has a tail. Point to the cat's tail. Name other animals that have a tail.* (children respond)

Listening to the Story

Redirect children's attention to the Day 1 page. Say: *Listen and look at the picture as I read a story about a cat and its parts.*

My cat Lulu has different parts that help her. She has black and brown fur that keeps her warm. She has a tiny pink nose that she uses to smell her food. Lulu has whiskers right next to her nose. Her whiskers help her feel things. She has two ears that move and twitch when she hears a noise. She also has four legs and four paws that help her run fast or creep slowly through the house. I love my cat Lulu.

Confirming Understanding

Distribute crayons or markers. Develop the science concept by asking children questions about the story. Ask:

• *How does the cat use her nose?* (to smell food) *Color her nose pink.*

• *How does the cat's fur help her?* (keeps her warm) *Make a black dot on her fur.*

• *How many ears does the cat have?* (two) *What do they help her do?* (hear) *Make a brown dot on each of the cat's ears.*

• *How many legs does the cat have?* (four) *Make a red dot on each leg.*

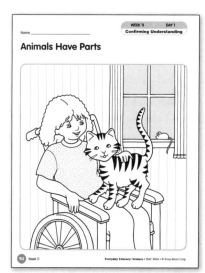

Day 1 picture

Life Science

• Represent observations of living things in a variety of ways

• Understand that people, animals, and plants are living things that have basic needs

Literacy

Oral Language Development

• Respond orally to simple questions

Comprehension

• Recall details

• Make connections using illustrations, prior knowledge, or real-life experiences

• Listen to stories being read aloud

Reinforcing the Concept

Reread the Day 1 story. Then reinforce this week's science concept by guiding a discussion about the story. Say:

Our story tells us about a cat's different parts. What parts does the cat have? (nose, whiskers, ears, fur, legs, paws, tail, etc.)

Distribute the Day 2 activity and crayons. Say:

• *Point to box 1. What do you see?* (a cat and an elephant) *Do both animals have parts? Color the happy face for* **yes** *or the sad face for* **no***.* (yes) *Are all of the cat's parts and the elephant's parts the same?* (No, the elephant doesn't have fur; The cat does not have a trunk; etc.)

• *Point to box 2. Do the cat and the horse both have tails? Color the happy face for* **yes** *or the sad face for* **no***.* (yes)

• *Point to box 3. Do the cat and the bird each have four legs? Color the happy face for* **yes** *or the sad face for* **no***.* (no)

• *Point to box 4. Do the cat and the lion each have whiskers? Color the happy face for* **yes** *or the sad face for* **no***.* (yes)

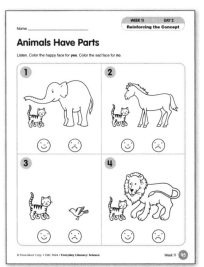

Day 2 activity

Life Science

• Represent observations of living things in a variety of ways

• Understand that people, animals, and plants are living things that have basic needs

Literacy

Oral Language Development

• Respond orally to simple questions

Comprehension

• Recall details

• Make connections using illustrations, prior knowledge, or real-life experiences

• Make inferences and draw conclusions

Developing the Concept

To introduce the activity, guide a discussion that helps children recall the Day 1 story. Say:

Lulu the cat has black and brown fur and a pink nose. She has ears, a tail, four paws, and whiskers. Do all animals have the same parts as Lulu? (No, different animals may have different parts.)

Distribute the Day 3 activity and crayons. Say:

• *An elephant uses its trunk to pick up food. Put your finger on the elephant. Which part is missing?* (nose or trunk) *Draw a line from the elephant to its trunk.*

• *A monkey uses its tail to swing from tree to tree. Put your finger on the monkey. Which part is missing?* (tail) *Draw a line from the monkey to its tail.*

• *A whale uses its tail to swim through the ocean. Put your finger on the whale. Which part is missing?* (tail) *Draw a line from the whale to its tail.*

• *A bat uses its wings to fly. Put your finger on the bat. Which part is missing?* (wings) *Draw a line from the bat to its wings.*

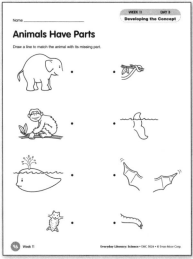

Day 3 activity

Life Science
• Represent observations of living things in a variety of ways
• Understand that people, animals, and plants are living things that have basic needs

Literacy

Oral Language Development
• Respond orally to simple questions

Comprehension
• Recall details
• Make connections using illustrations, prior knowledge, or real-life experiences
• Make inferences and draw conclusions

Applying the Concept

Introduce the activity by saying:

Animals have different parts that help them do things, such as move from place to place.

• *Some animals have legs that help them walk, run, and jump.*

• *Some animals have wings that help them fly.*

• *Some animals have fins that help them swim.*

Distribute the Day 4 activity and crayons. Say:

• *Point to the first picture. What does it show?* (a bird) *How does a bird move?* (It flies or hops.) *What body parts help a bird fly?* (wings) *Circle the bird's wings.*

• *Point to picture 2. What does it show?* (a fish) *How does a fish move?* (It swims.) *What body parts help a fish swim?* (fins) *Circle a fin.*

• *Point to picture 3. What does it show?* (a zebra) *How does a zebra move?* (walks, runs) *What body parts help a zebra walk?* (legs) *Circle two of the zebra's legs.*

• *Point to picture 4. What does it show?* (a monkey) *How does a monkey move?* (walks, swings) *What body parts help a monkey swing?* (arms, legs, tail) *Circle one of the body parts that helps a monkey move.*

Day 4 activity

Life Science
• Represent observations of living things in a variety of ways
• Understand that people, animals, and plants are living things that have basic needs
• Explore characteristics of living things

Scientific Thinking & Inquiry
• Gather and record information through simple observations and investigations

Home–School Connection p. 98
Spanish version available (see p. 2)

Hands-on Science Activity

Reinforce this week's science concept with the following hands-on activity:

Materials: a collection of small plastic toy animals, stuffed animals, or pictures of animals; several sheets of different-colored paper for sorting mats

Preparation: Place sorting mats on a flat surface.

Activity: Have children sort animals into groups based on similar parts. Guide the sorting by asking questions such as:

• *Which animals have fur?*

• *Which animals have two legs? four? none?*

• *Which animals have a tail? no tail?*

• *Which animals have paws? fins? feet and toes?*

• *Which animals have wings? feathers?*

• *Which animals have a long neck? short neck?*

• *Which animals have whiskers?*

Name _____

Animals Have Parts

Everyday Literacy: Science • EMC 5024 • © Evan-Moor Corp.

Name _____

Animals Have Parts

Listen. Color the happy face for **yes**. Color the sad face for **no**.

Name _____

Animals Have Parts

Draw a line to match the animal with its missing part.

   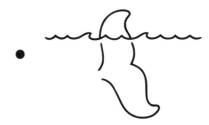

   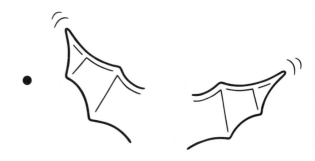

Animals Have Parts

Circle the parts that help the animal move.

Name _____

What I Learned

What to Do

Have your child look at each picture below. Ask your child to compare each pair of animals, telling which parts they have that are the same and which are different. Ask: *Do they have the same noses? The same ears? Do they each have fur, tails, wings, or whiskers? Do they have the same number of legs?* Then have your child color the pictures.

Science Concept: Animals have body parts.

To Parents

This week your child learned that animals have different body parts.

What to Do Next

Have your child act out the movements of various animals. Point to an animal on this page and have your child decide how it moves (fly, walk, gallop, etc.) and demonstrate it for you.

Everyday Literacy: Science • EMC 5024 • © Evan-Moor Corp.

Concept

Living things grow and change.

Living and Nonliving Things

Science Objective:
To help children understand that living things grow, but nonliving things do not

Science Vocabulary:
change, grow, living, nonliving, pumpkin, rock, seeds, sprout

Day 1
SKILLS

Life Science

• Represent observations of living things in a variety of ways

• Understand that people, animals, and plants are living things that have basic needs

Literacy

Oral Language Development

• Respond orally to simple questions

Comprehension

• Recall details

• Make connections using illustrations, prior knowledge, or real-life experiences

• Listen to stories being read aloud

• Make inferences and draw conclusions

Introducing the Concept

Distribute the Day 1 activity page to each child and point to each item in the picture as you talk about it. Say:

Let's look at this picture to find things that grow and change and things that do not.

• *These are pumpkin plants. Do plants grow and change?* (yes) *Plants are living things. Living things grow and change. This is a boy. Do boys grow and change?* (yes) *Boys are living things, too. They grow and change.*

• *This is a rock. Is a rock a living thing?* (no) *That's right, a rock is not a living thing. It does not grow. It is nonliving.*

Continue the process with the animals, garden tools, and trees.

Listening to the Story

Prepare children to listen to the story. Say: *Listen and look at the picture as I read a story about a boy who has living and nonliving things in his backyard.*

There are living and nonliving things in Joel's backyard. There are pumpkin plants. They started out as seeds. The seeds grew into little sprouts. The sprouts grew into plants with leaves and flowers. Soon the flowers changed into pumpkins! Living things are fun to watch! There are also rocks in Joel's backyard. Rocks are not living things. Rocks do not grow. But they are good to sit on!

Confirming Understanding

Distribute crayons or markers. Reinforce the science concept by asking children questions about the story. Ask:

• *What was growing in the boy's backyard?* (pumpkin plants) *Are pumpkin plants living or nonliving?* (living) *How do you know?* (because they grow and change) *Color one pumpkin orange.*

• *What is the boy sitting on?* (a rock) *Are rocks living or nonliving?* (nonliving) *How do you know?* (because they do not grow) *Color the rock brown.*

Day 1 picture

Life Science

• Represent observations of living things in a variety of ways

• Understand that people, animals, and plants are living things that have basic needs

Literacy

Oral Language Development

• Respond orally to simple questions

Comprehension

• Recall details

• Make connections using illustrations, prior knowledge, or real-life experiences

• Listen to stories being read aloud

• Make inferences and draw conclusions

Reinforcing the Concept

Reread the Day 1 story. Then reinforce this week's science concept by guiding a discussion about the story. Say:

Our story tells about living and nonliving things.

- *What living things were in the boy's backyard?* (pumpkin plants, squirrel, bird, trees)

Distribute the Day 2 activity and crayons. Say:

- *Point to box 1. Is the boy sitting on something that is living? Color the happy face for* **yes** *or the sad face for* **no**. (no) *What is he sitting on?* (a rock)

- *Point to box 2. Is the girl holding something living? Color the happy face for* **yes** *or the sad face for* **no**. (yes) *What is she holding?* (a puppy) *Can a puppy grow?* (yes)

- *Point to box 3. Is the boy holding something that is living? Color the happy face for* **yes** *or the sad face for* **no**. (no) *How do you know a wheelbarrow is nonliving?* (It doesn't grow.)

- *Point to box 4. Is the boy watering something that is living? Color the happy face for* **yes** *or the sad face for* **no**. (yes) *How do you know the pumpkin plant is living?* (It is growing in the garden.)

Day 2 activity

Life Science

• Represent observations of living things in a variety of ways

• Understand that people, animals, and plants are living things that have basic needs

Literacy

Oral Language Development

• Respond orally to simple questions

Comprehension

• Make connections using illustrations, prior knowledge, or real-life experiences

• Make inferences and draw conclusions

Identifying the Concept

Distribute the Day 3 activity and crayons. Then introduce the activity by saying:

Living and nonliving things are all around us. Look around the room. Name one thing that is living and one thing that is nonliving. (children respond)

- *Now look at the top picture. What* **living** *things do you see?* (girl, bird, tree, flowers, grass) *Circle each living thing.*

- *Now look at the bottom picture. What* **nonliving** *things do you see?* (tractor, scarecrow, fence) *Circle each nonliving thing.*

Day 3 activity

Guide a discussion about the pictures that children circled. Say:

- *How do you know that the girl, the bird, the tree, the flowers, and the grass are living?* (They grow and change.) *How might a bird change?* (e.g., hatches from egg, gets bigger, learns to fly)

- *Now let's talk about the nonliving things. How do you know that the tractor, the scarecrow, and the fence are nonliving?* (They do not grow.)

<table>
<tr><td>

Day 4
SKILLS

Life Science
- Represent observations of living things in a variety of ways
- Understand that people, animals, and plants are living things that have basic needs

Literacy

Oral Language Development
- Respond orally to simple questions

Comprehension
- Make connections using illustrations, prior knowledge, or real-life experiences
- Make inferences and draw conclusions

</td></tr>
</table>

Applying the Concept

Distribute the Day 4 activity and crayons. Then introduce the activity by saying:

People, animals, and plants are living things that change and grow.

- *Point to the picture of the sprout. A sprout is a baby plant. Is a sprout living or nonliving? (living) What will the sprout look like when it grows and changes? (a plant) Draw a line from the sprout to the picture that shows a pumpkin plant.*

- *Point to the picture of the puppy. Is a puppy living or nonliving? (living) What will it look like when it grows and changes? (a big dog) Draw a line from the puppy to the picture that shows a big dog.*

- *Point to the picture of the young tree. Is a tree living or nonliving? (living) What will it look like when it grows and changes? (a tall tree) Draw a line from the young tree to the picture that shows a tall tree.*

- *Point to the picture of the baby. Is a baby living or nonliving? (living) What will it look like when it grows and changes? (a boy) Draw a line from the baby to the picture that shows a boy.*

Day 4 activity

Day 5
SKILLS

Life Science
- Represent observations of living things in a variety of ways
- Understand that people, animals, and plants are living things that have basic needs

Scientific Thinking & Inquiry
- Gather and record information through simple observations and investigations

Home–School Connection p. 106
Spanish version available (see p. 2)

Hands-on Science Activity

Reinforce this week's science concept with the following hands-on activity:

Materials: clip art or magazine pictures of plants, animals, people, and a variety of nonliving objects; bulletin board paper, marker, and glue sticks

Preparation: Use the marker to draw a line down the middle of a sheet of bulletin board paper. Label one half **Living** and the other half **Nonliving**. Next to each label, attach a picture that shows an example of it.

Activity: Have children sort the pictures and glue them onto the chart in the correct columns. Discuss each picture as it is placed. Have children name each object, plant, animal, or person and tell why they think it is living or nonliving.

Name _____

Living and Nonliving Things

Name _____

Living and Nonliving Things

Listen. Color the happy face for **yes**. Color the sad face for **no**.

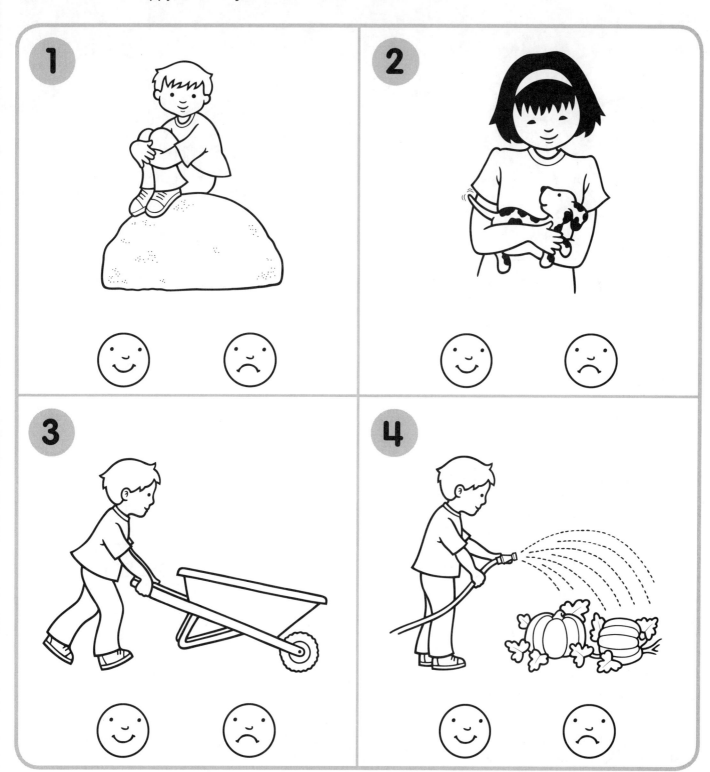

Name _____

Living and Nonliving Things

Listen. Circle the **living** things in the top picture. Circle the **nonliving** things in the bottom picture.

Name _____

Living and Nonliving Things

Listen. Draw a line to match.

1

2

3

4

Name _____

What I Learned

What to Do

Have your child look at the picture below. Ask your child to point to and name the living things. Then have him or her point to and name the nonliving things.

Science Concept: Living things grow and change.

To Parents

This week your child learned that living things grow and change and that nonliving things do not grow.

What to Do Next

Play a game with your child. Name an object, plant, animal, or person in the room. Have your child go to the object, touch it, and say *living* or *nonliving* to describe it.

People Grow and Change

Science Objective:
To help children understand that people are living beings who grow and change

Science Vocabulary:
baby, body, changing, growing, hair, talk, teeth, walk

Day 1
SKILLS

Life Science

• Represent observations of living things in a variety of ways

• Understand that people, animals, and plants are living things that have basic needs

Literacy

Oral Language Development

• Respond orally to simple questions

Comprehension

• Recall details

• Make connections using illustrations, prior knowledge, or real-life experiences

• Listen to stories being read aloud

• Make inferences and draw conclusions

Introducing the Concept

Distribute the Day 1 activity page and point to the picture as you talk about it. Say:

People are living beings. You and I are living beings. We grow and change. This picture shows a little girl eating breakfast. She is eating cereal. Look at the little picture beside the girl. It shows her when she was a baby. She drank from a bottle when she was a baby.

• *Have you grown and changed since you were a baby?* (yes) *Tell me one way you have grown and changed.* (children respond)

Listening to the Story

Redirect children's attention to the Day 1 page. Say: *Listen and look at the picture as I read a story about a little girl who is growing and changing.*

My name is Lisa. I am growing and changing every day. That is my baby picture. I had hardly any hair when I was a baby! I didn't have any teeth, either. I didn't know how to walk or talk. When I was hungry, I cried until my mom fed me with a bottle. My parents did everything for me. But now I am six years old. My body has grown, my hair has grown, and I have teeth! I can walk, talk, and help make my own breakfast. I am so glad I am growing—I can't wait to be seven!

Confirming Understanding

Distribute crayons or markers. Reinforce the science concept by asking children questions about the story. Ask:

• *Has Lisa's hair changed since she was a baby?* (yes) *How has it changed?* (It has grown longer.) *Color Lisa's hair brown.*

• *Did Lisa have teeth when she was a baby?* (no) *Does she have teeth now that she is six years old?* (yes) *Color something Lisa can chew with her teeth.*

• *Why can Lisa walk and talk now?* (Her body grew and changed.) *Do you think she will keep growing and changing?* (yes)

Day 1 picture

Life Science

- Represent observations of living things in a variety of ways
- Understand that people, animals, and plants are living things that have basic needs

Literacy

Oral Language Development

- Respond orally to simple questions

Comprehension

- Recall details
- Make connections using illustrations, prior knowledge, or real-life experiences
- Listen to stories being read aloud
- Make inferences and draw conclusions

Reinforcing the Concept

Reread the Day 1 story. Then reinforce this week's science concept by guiding a discussion about the story. Say:

Our story tells us that people grow and change. Lisa's body changed from a baby into a six-year-old girl. What parts of her body changed? (Her hair grew longer; Her legs and arms grew longer; She grew teeth; etc.)

Distribute the Day 2 activity and crayons. Say:

- *Point to box 1. Does the picture show Lisa when she was a little girl or a baby?* (baby) *Does the baby have long hair and a mouth full of teeth? Color the happy face for* **yes** *or the sad face for* **no**. (no)

- *Now look at box 2. Does the picture show Lisa as a little girl or a baby?* (little girl) *Lisa used to be a baby. Has Lisa grown and changed? Color the happy face for* **yes** *or the sad face for* **no**. (yes)

- *Look at box 3. Can the baby make herself a bottle of milk to drink? Color the happy face for* **yes** *or the sad face for* **no**. (no) *Why can't the baby make herself a bottle?* (She cannot walk or get things on her own.)

- *Look at box 4. Does Lisa help fix her own breakfast? Color the happy face for* **yes** *or the sad face for* **no**. (yes) *Why can Lisa help make her own breakfast now that she is six?* (She can walk and talk and get things on her own.)

Day 2 activity

Life Science

- Represent observations of living things in a variety of ways
- Understand that people, animals, and plants are living things that have basic needs

Literacy

Oral Language Development

- Respond orally to simple questions

Comprehension

- Make connections using illustrations, prior knowledge, or real-life experiences
- Make inferences and draw conclusions

Developing the Concept

Distribute the Day 3 activity and crayons. Then introduce the activity by saying:

You used to be a baby. Your body has grown and changed. Now you are a child. Listen to this story about a baby boy who is growing and changing:

- *Marcus is a little baby. He wears diapers and drinks a bottle. His parents feed him and take care of him. Which picture shows Marcus as a little baby? Draw a line from the number 1 to that picture.*

- *Now Marcus is two years old. He can walk and drink from a cup. He likes to play with toys. Which picture shows Marcus as a two-year-old? Draw a line from the number 2 to that picture.*

- *Marcus has grown older. He is four years old now. He runs and plays outside. He talks to his friends at preschool. He helps his mom and dad at home. Which picture shows Marcus as a four-year-old? Draw a line from the number 3 to that picture.*

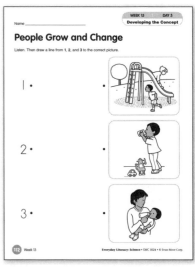

Day 3 activity

Life Science

- Represent observations of living things in a variety of ways
- Understand that people, animals, and plants are living things that have basic needs

Literacy

Oral Language Development

- Respond orally to simple questions

Comprehension

- Make inferences and draw conclusions
- Make connections using illustrations, prior knowledge, or real-life experiences

Applying the Concept

Distribute the Day 4 activity and crayons. Then introduce the activity by saying:

People are living beings that grow and change.

Day 4 activity

- *Point to picture 1. Who does it show?* (a baby boy) *Will this baby boy grow and change?* (yes) *Draw a line to the picture that shows how he has grown and changed. What is he doing now that he could not do when he was a baby?* (running, playing outside)

- *Point to picture 2. Who does it show?* (a little girl) *Will this little girl grow and change?* (yes) *Draw a line to the picture that shows how she has grown and changed. What is she doing now that she could not do when she was a little girl?* (riding a bicycle without training wheels)

- *Point to picture 3. Who does it show?* (a baby girl) *Will this baby girl grow and change?* (yes) *Draw a line to the picture that shows how she has grown and changed. What is she doing now that she could not do when she was a baby?* (eating solid food, drinking from a cup)

- *Point to picture 4. Who does it show?* (a little boy) *Will this boy grow and change?* (yes) *Draw a line to the picture that shows how he has grown and changed. What is he doing now that he could not do when he was a little boy?* (dunking a basketball)

Life Science

- Represent observations of living things in a variety of ways
- Understand that people, animals, and plants are living things that have basic needs

Scientific Thinking & Inquiry

- Gather information through the use of one or more of the senses
- Gather and record information through simple observations and investigations

Home–School Connection p. 114
Spanish version available (see p. 2)

Hands-on Science Activity

Reinforce this week's science concept with the following hands-on activity:

Materials: masking tape, large plastic hoop, and two or three beanbags

Preparation: Create an activity course that includes a "balance beam" and a beanbag toss. For the balance beam, place a 5-foot line of masking tape on the ground. For the beanbag toss, place beanbags near the end of the balance beam. Lay a hoop on the ground about two feet from the beanbags.

Activity: Tell children that they can do many things they couldn't do when they were babies: stand, walk, hop, toss, etc. Invite children to use these skills to complete the course in different ways. For example:

- walking on the balance beam, placing one foot in front of the other
- hopping on the balance beam all the way to the end and then picking up the beanbags and tossing them into the hoop

Allow one child at a time to complete the course.

Name _____

People Grow and Change

Name _____

People Grow and Change

Listen. Color the happy face for **yes**. Color the sad face for **no**.

People Grow and Change

Listen. Then draw a line from **1**, **2**, and **3** to the correct picture.

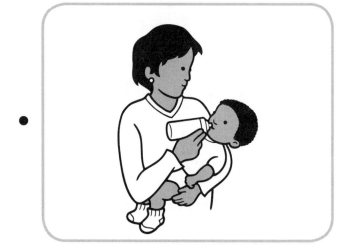

Name _____

People Grow and Change

Listen. Draw a line to match.

1

2

3

4

Name _____

What I Learned

What to Do
Have your child look at each of the pictures below. Ask him or her if the pictures show how a person changes and grows. Then have your child explain why or why not.

Science Concept: Living things grow and change.

To Parents
This week your child learned that people are living beings who grow and change.

What to Do Next
Have your child name things he or she can do now that he or she couldn't do as a baby and then pantomime them.

Everyday Literacy: Science • EMC 5024 • © Evan-Moor Corp.

We Need the Sun

Science Objective:
To help children understand that the sun is an object in our sky that gives us light and heat

Science Vocabulary:
dark, Earth, heat, light, sky, sun, sunlight, weather

Day 1 SKILLS

Earth Science
- Represent observations about Earth and space

in a variety of ways
- Explore properties of Earth and space
- Understand that the sun, moon, and stars are objects in our sky
- Understand that the sun gives Earth light and heat

Literacy

Oral Language Development
- Respond orally to simple questions

Comprehension
- Recall details
- Make connections using illustrations, prior knowledge, or real-life experiences
- Listen to stories being read aloud
- Make inferences and draw conclusions

Introducing the Concept

Activate students' prior knowledge about the sun by saying:

Every day the sun comes up. It lights up the sky. It warms the air.

- *Have you played outside on a sunny day?* (yes) *What did the weather feel like?* (warm) *Was the sky light or dark?* (light) *The sun gives us heat and light. It warms us. We need the sun to live.*

- *Do you think animals and plants need the sun, too?* (yes) *Sunlight helps animals stay warm. Sunlight helps plants grow. And animals eat plants.*

Listening to the Story

Distribute the Day 1 activity page to each child. Say: *Listen and look at the picture as I read a story about how the sun gives us light and heat.*

One summer day, Cody went swimming. After he got out of the water, he lay on his towel in the sunshine. The warmth of the sun dried Cody's swimsuit and his body. He thought about what his teacher told him about the sun. She told him that without sunlight, the Earth would be cold and dark. She explained that the sun gives us heat and light. Without the sun, people, plants, and animals could not live on Earth. Cody was glad it was a sunny day, because without the sun, he'd be cold and wet instead of warm and dry!

Confirming Understanding

Distribute crayons or markers. Reinforce the science concept by asking children questions about the story. Ask:

- *How did the sunshine help Cody after swimming?* (It dried his swimsuit and his body; It made him feel warm.) *Color Cody's swimsuit green.*

- *What does the sun give us?* (light and heat) *Color the sun yellow.*

- *Could people, plants, and animals live on Earth without the sun?* (no) *Make an **X** on the tree and the squirrel.*

Day 1 picture

Earth Science

- Represent observations about Earth and space in a variety of ways
- Explore properties of Earth and space
- Understand that the sun, moon, and stars are objects in our sky
- Understand that the sun gives Earth light and heat

Literacy

Oral Language Development

- Respond orally to simple questions

Comprehension

- Recall details
- Make connections using illustrations, prior knowledge, or real-life experiences
- Listen to stories being read aloud

Reinforcing the Concept

Reread the Day 1 story. Then reinforce this week's science concept by guiding a discussion about the story. Say:

Our story tells us that without the sun, people, plants, and animals could not live on Earth. What does the sun give us? (light and heat)

Distribute the Day 2 activity and crayons. Say:

- *Point to box 1. Look at the two pictures. Which one needs the sun—Cody or the beach ball?* (Cody) *Draw a line from the sun to Cody.*

- *Point to box 2. Look at the two pictures. Which one needs the sun—the fence or the tree?* (tree) *Draw a line from the sun to the tree.*

- *Point to box 3. Look at the two pictures. Which one needs the sun— the cat bed or the cat?* (cat) *Draw a line from the sun to the cat.*

- *Point to box 4. Look at the two pictures. Which one needs the sun— the flower or the bike?* (flower) *Draw a line from the sun to the flower.*

Day 2 activity

Earth Science

- Represent observations about Earth and space in a variety of ways
- Explore properties of Earth and space
- Understand that the sun, moon, and stars are objects in our sky
- Understand that the sun gives Earth light and heat

Literacy

Oral Language Development

- Respond orally to simple questions

Comprehension

- Recall details
- Make connections using illustrations, prior knowledge, or real-life experiences

Developing the Concept

Distribute the Day 3 activity and crayons. Then introduce the activity by saying:

Sunlight helps plants grow. People eat plants. Animals eat plants. Look at the picture. It shows how the sun helps people and animals get food.

- *Point to the orange tree. Does a tree need sunlight to grow?* (yes) *Do people eat oranges?* (yes) *Use an orange crayon to color one orange.*

- *Point to the boy. Does the boy need sunlight?* (yes) *The sun helps plants to grow. The boy is eating a tomato sandwich. Does a tomato grow on a plant?* (yes) *Circle the boy's sandwich.*

- *Point to the rabbit. Does an animal need sunlight?* (yes) *The rabbit needs sunlight to keep warm. The rabbit also needs food. Sunlight helps carrots grow. The rabbit eats the carrots. Make a pink dot on the rabbit. Color the top of one carrot green.*

Have children finish coloring the picture.

Day 3 activity

Earth Science

• Represent observations about Earth and space in a variety of ways

• Explore properties of Earth and space

• Understand that the sun, moon, and stars are objects in our sky

• Understand that the sun gives Earth light and heat

Literacy

Oral Language Development

• Respond orally to simple questions

Comprehension

• Recall details

• Make connections using illustrations, prior knowledge, or real-life experiences

Applying the Concept

Introduce the activity by saying:

The sun is always in the sky even if we can't see it. We begin to see the sun's light in the morning. We see more of the sun's light during the day. We don't see the sun's light at night.

• *Is it light or dark outside when you wake up in the morning?* (answers vary)

• *Is it light or dark outside when you are at school?* (light)

• *Is it light or dark outside when you go to bed at night?* (answers vary)

Day 4 activity

Distribute the Day 4 activity and crayons. Say:

• *Point to row 1. Maria just woke up. It is morning. The sun rises in the morning and lights up the sky. Point to the sun rising. Color the sun yellow.*

• *Point to row 2. Maria is playing at school. It is afternoon. The sun is high in the sky in the afternoon. Point to the sun high in the sky. Color the sun yellow. Color the sky blue.*

• *Point to row 3. Maria is eating dinner. It is nighttime. The sun is setting in the sky. It is getting dark outside. Point to the sun setting. Color the sun yellow.*

Earth Science

• Represent observations about Earth and space in a variety of ways

• Explore properties of Earth and space

• Understand that the sun, moon, and stars are objects in our sky

• Understand that the sun gives Earth light and heat

Scientific Thinking & Inquiry

• Gather and record information through simple observations and investigations

Home–School Connection p. 122
Spanish version available (see p. 2)

Hands-on Science Activity

Reinforce this week's science concept with the following hands-on activity:

Living	Nonliving
☼	

Materials: one sheet of white construction paper for each child, crayons, glue sticks, scissors, and clip art or magazines that contain pictures of plants, animals, people, and nonliving objects

Preparation: Draw a line down the center of each sheet of construction paper. Label one side **Living** and the other side **Nonliving**. Place all the pictures where children can easily access them. Distribute one sheet of construction paper, crayons, a glue stick, and a pair of scissors to each child.

Activity: Introduce the activity by saying:

*People, plants, and animals are living things. **Living** things need the sun.*

• *Draw a sun on this side of the paper under the word **Living**. We are going to find pictures of living things and glue them under the sun.*

• *Nonliving things do <u>not</u> need the sun. We are going to find pictures of nonliving things and glue them under the word **Nonliving**.*

Name _____

We Need the Sun

Name _____

We Need the Sun

Draw a line from the sun to the thing that needs it.

1

2

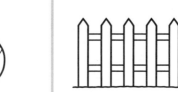 

3

4

Name _____

We Need the Sun

Listen and follow the directions.

Everyday Literacy: Science • EMC 5024 • © Evan-Moor Corp.

Name _____

We Need the Sun

Listen and follow the directions.

1

 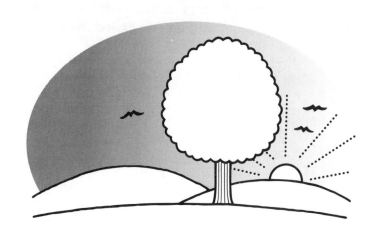

2

 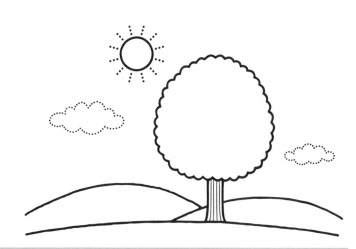

3

Name _____

What I Learned

What to Do
Have your child look at the picture below and point out all the things that need the sun to live. Ask him or her to tell you why each person, animal, or plant needs the sun to live. Then have your child color all the things that need the sun.

Science Concept: The sun is an object in our sky.

To Parents
This week your child learned that the sun is an object in our sky that gives us light and heat.

What to Do Next
Do an experiment with your child. Plant one seed in a pot and set it on a windowsill. Plant another seed in a pot and set it in a part of the house that does not receive sunlight. Water both plants. Watch the progress of both seeds. Discuss with your child why one seed grew and the other did not.

Everyday Literacy: Science • EMC 5024 • © Evan-Moor Corp.

Day and Night

Science Objective:
To help children understand that the Earth spins around, and that this is why we have day and night

Science Vocabulary:
day, Earth, night, shine, spin, sun

Day 1
SKILLS

Earth Science

• Represent observations about Earth and space in a variety of ways

• Explore properties of Earth and space

• Understand that the sun, moon, and stars are objects in our sky

• Understand that the Earth spins

Literacy

Oral Language Development

• Respond orally to simple questions

Comprehension

• Recall details

• Make connections using illustrations, prior knowledge, or real-life experiences

• Listen to stories being read aloud

• Make inferences and draw conclusions

Introducing the Concept

Begin by activating children's prior knowledge about the difference between day and night. Ask:

• *Do we see the sun at night or during the day?* (day) *What does the sky look like on a sunny day?* (bright, blue, etc.)

• *Do we see the sun at night?* (no) *What does the sky look like at night?* (dark, stars, moon)

Then introduce children to the concept of what causes day and night. Say:

We live on Earth. Earth is like a big ball that spins around. It spins slowly, so we can't feel it. The sun is always shining on Earth, but we can't always see it.

Listening to the Story

Distribute the Day 1 activity page to each child. Say: *Listen and look at the picture as I read a story about why the Earth has day and night.*

During the day, we see the sun. At night, we do not see it. Does the sun stop shining at night? No! Then why can't we see the sun at night? The Earth is round like a big ball. It spins around slowly. When our side of the Earth faces the sun, it is day. The other side of Earth is dark. It is night there. The Earth keeps turning around and around. So, sometimes it is day where we are and sometimes it is night.

Confirming Understanding

Distribute crayons or markers. Reinforce the science concept by asking children questions about the story. Ask:

• *What shines down on Earth from the sky?* (the sun) *Color the sun yellow.*

• *The Earth is like a big ball. Does the Earth stay still or does it spin around?* (It spins around.) *Draw a line under the picture of the Earth.*

• *Does our side of the Earth face the sun during the day or at night?* (during the day) *Color the* **day** *side of the Earth blue.*

Day 1 picture

Day 2
SKILLS

Earth Science

- Represent observations about Earth and space in a variety of ways
- Explore properties of Earth and space
- Understand that the sun, moon, and stars are objects in our sky
- Understand that the Earth spins

Literacy

Oral Language Development

- Respond orally to simple questions

Comprehension

- Recall details
- Make connections using illustrations, prior knowledge, or real-life experiences
- Make inferences and draw conclusions

Reinforcing the Concept

Reread the Day 1 story. Then reinforce this week's science concept by guiding a discussion about the story. Say:

Our story tells us that Earth has day and night. How does the sky look during the day? How does the sky look at night? (children respond)

Distribute the Day 2 activity and crayons. Allow children to mark their answers each time before asking the next question. Say:

- *Point to box 1. When do we see the sun shining? Day or night?* (day) *Make an **X** on the side of the Earth where it is **day**.*

- *Point to box 2. When it is dark outside, is it day or night?* (night) *Make an **X** on the side of the Earth where it is **night**.*

- *Point to box 3. Does the sun spin around the Earth? Color the happy face for **yes** or the sad face for **no**.* (no)

- *Point to box 4. Does the sun shine everywhere on Earth at the same time? Color the happy face for **yes** or the sad face for **no**.* (no)

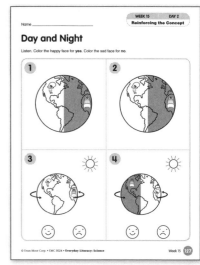

Day 2 activity

Day 3
SKILLS

Earth Science

- Represent observations about Earth and space in a variety of ways
- Explore properties of Earth and space
- Understand that the sun, moon, and stars are objects in our sky
- Understand that the Earth spins

Literacy

Oral Language Development

- Respond orally to simple questions

Comprehension

- Make connections using illustrations, prior knowledge, or real-life experiences
- Make inferences and draw conclusions

Developing the Concept

To introduce the activity, guide a discussion that helps children recall the Day 1 story. Say:

We learned that we have day and night because the Earth spins around.

- *What do you see in the sky during the day?* (sun)

- *What do you see in the sky at night?* (stars, moon)

Distribute the Day 3 activity and crayons. Say:

- *This picture shows night and day. Look at the part of the picture that shows night. What is the boy doing?* (sleeping in bed) *Circle the bed. What nighttime animal is in the tree outside?* (owl) *Draw a line under the owl. What is shining in the sky?* (stars) *What else do we sometimes see in the sky at night?* (moon) *Draw the moon in the sky.*

- *Look at the part of the picture that shows day. What is the boy doing?* (playing basketball) *Draw a line under the boy. What is the dad doing?* (mowing the grass) *What do you see in the sky during the day?* (sun) *Draw the sun in the sky.*

Day 3 activity

Earth Science
• Represent observations about Earth and space in a variety of ways
• Explore properties of Earth and space
• Understand that the sun, moon, and stars are objects in our sky
• Understand that the Earth spins

Literacy

Oral Language Development
• Respond orally to simple questions

Comprehension
• Recall details
• Make connections using illustrations, prior knowledge, or real-life experiences
• Make inferences and draw conclusions

Applying the Concept

Help children recall the Day 1 story. Say:

The Earth is like a big ball that keeps spinning around. When our side faces the sun, we have day. The other side has night.

> • *What are some things you do during the day?* (children respond)
>
> • *What do you do at night?* (children respond)

Distribute the Day 4 activity and crayons. Point to each picture as you name it. Say:

> • *Point to the first box in the middle of the page. What does the picture show?* (sun)
> *Point to the second box. What does the picture show?* (moon)
>
> • *Now look at the other pictures. Point to the picture of the children at preschool. Do you go to preschool during the day or night?* (day)
> *Draw a line from the children at preschool to the picture of the sun.*
>
> • *Point to the picture of a boy playing catch. Do you play catch during the day or night?* (day) *Draw a line from the boy playing catch to the picture of the sun.*

Repeat the process with each picture.

Day 4 activity

Earth Science
• Represent observations about Earth and space in a variety of ways
• Explore properties of Earth and space
• Understand that the sun, moon, and stars are objects in our sky
• Understand that the Earth spins

Scientific Thinking & Inquiry
• Gather and record information through simple observations and investigations

Hands-on Science Activity

Materials: ball, flashlight, and masking tape

Preparation: This activity should be done in a room that can be darkened.

Activity: Help children visualize how the Earth spins and how the sun shines on only one side at a time, creating day and night. Place a small piece of masking tape on the ball as a marker to represent your location on Earth. In a darkened room, hold the ball (Earth) so the children can see the marker pointed toward them. Have a child stand about six feet away from you and shine the flashlight (sun) on the ball. Have the children tell you if they see the sun shining on their part of the Earth. Ask: *Is it day or night?* (day) Then turn the ball so the marker is toward you and away from the flashlight. Ask: *Is it day or night?* (night)

Play a game by having the children close their eyes. Turn the ball to show either day or night where they are and have them open their eyes. If it shows day, they stand up. If it shows night, they sit down. Repeat the game.

Home–School Connection p. 130
Spanish version available (see p. 2)

Name _____

Day and Night

Name _____

Day and Night

Listen. Color the happy face for **yes**. Color the sad face for **no**.

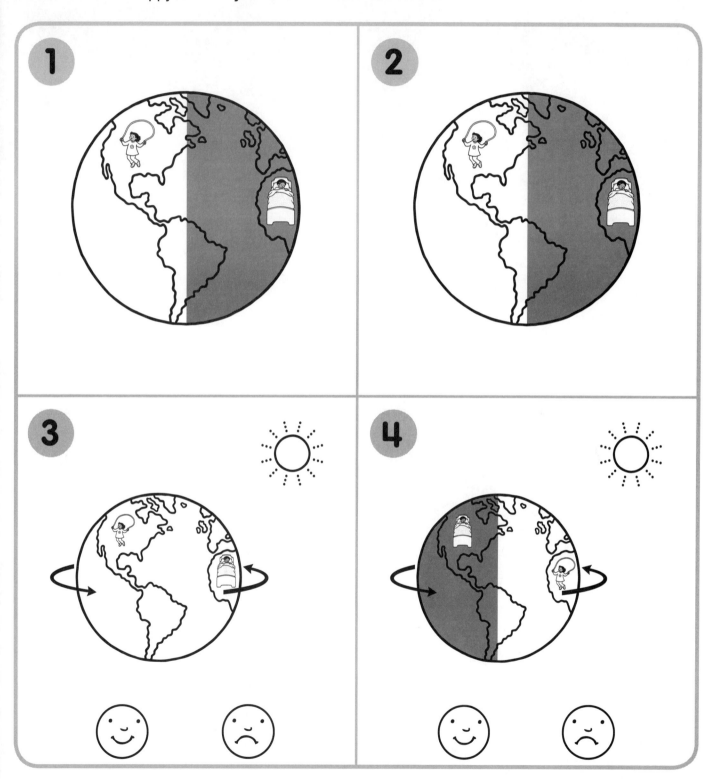

Name _____

Day and Night

Listen and follow the directions.

Everyday Literacy: Science • EMC 5024 • © Evan-Moor Corp.

Name _____

Day and Night

Match the activity to show when you do it—**day** or **night**.

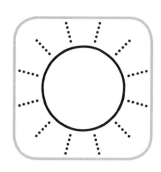

Name _____

What I Learned

What to Do

Have your child look at the picture below. Ask him or her to point to the Earth and the sun. Ask: *Which one spins slowly around?* (Earth) *What happens when the Earth spins?* (The sky changes from day to night.) Have your child tell you which child is on the day side of Earth and which one is on the night side.

Science Concept: The Earth has day and night.

To Parents

This week your child learned that the Earth spins around, making day and night.

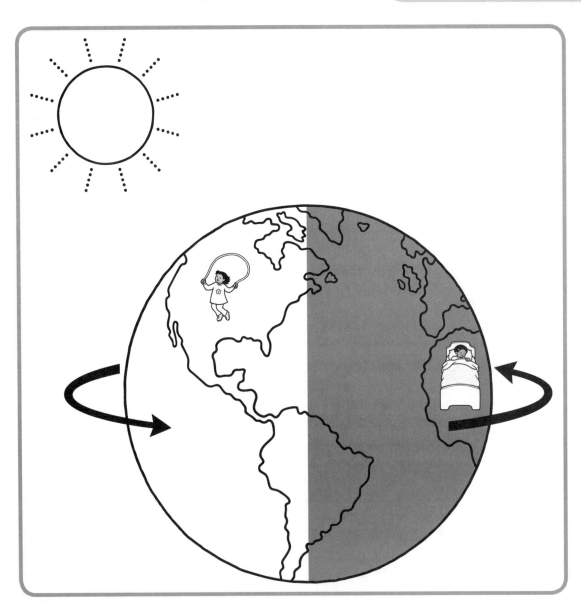

What to Do Next

Help your child make a two-column chart with one side labeled "Day" and the other side labeled "Night." Then, in the correct column, have your child draw pictures of things he or she does during the day and things he or she does at night.

Everyday Literacy: Science • EMC 5024 • © Evan-Moor Corp.

WEEK 16

Concept

The moon is an object in our sky that does not change shape.

The Moon

Science Objective:
To help children understand that the moon is an object in our sky that is lit up by the sun and appears to change shape

Science Vocabulary:
crescent, dark, full, half, lit, moon, quarter, rock, shape, shines, sky, sun

Day 1 SKILLS

Earth Science

- Represent observations about Earth and space in a variety of ways
- Explore properties of Earth and space
- Understand that the sun, moon, and stars are objects in our sky
- Understand that the moon does not change shape

Literacy

Oral Language Development

- Respond orally to simple questions

Comprehension

- Recall details
- Make connections using illustrations, prior knowledge, or real-life experiences
- Listen to stories being read aloud
- Make inferences and draw conclusions

Introducing the Concept

Activate children's prior knowledge about the moon by saying:
The moon is an object in our sky. It is a big ball made of rock.

- *Have you looked up at the moon at night? (yes) What color was the moon? (white, yellow, silver, etc.) The moon looks like that because the sun shines on the moon and lights it up.*
- *Does the moon always look round like a ball? (No, sometimes it looks like a banana, sometimes it looks like a half circle, etc.) The sun shines on the moon in different ways and makes the moon look like it changes shape, but the moon does not change shape.*

Listening to the Story

Redirect children's attention to the Day 1 page. Say: *Listen and look at the pictures as I read a story about a girl who watches the moon every night.*

Every night, I look for the moon in the sky. The moon is a big ball of rock. The sun shines on the moon and lights it up. The moon is always a ball, but to me it seems to change shape. That's because I can see only the part of the moon that is lit. The other part is in darkness. Some nights, I can't see the moon at all. But it is still there in the sky!

Confirming Understanding

Distribute a blue crayon or marker. Reinforce the science concept by asking children questions about the pictures. Say:

- *Look at picture 1. What shape is the moon? (a circle) When the moon looks round, we call it a full moon. Circle the full moon.*
- *Look at picture 2. What does the moon look like? (part, or half, of a circle) It is called a quarter moon. Color the quarter moon.*
- *Look at picture 3. What shape does the moon look like? (a banana) It is called a crescent moon. Color the crescent moon.*
- *Look at picture 4. Can we see the part of the moon that is lit up? (no) No, we cannot see the part of the moon that is lit up, but it is there.*

Day 1 picture

Day 2
SKILLS

Earth Science

• Represent observations about Earth and space in a variety of ways

• Explore properties of Earth and space

• Understand that the sun, moon, and stars are objects in our sky

• Understand that the moon does not change shape

Literacy

Oral Language Development

• Respond orally to simple questions

Comprehension

• Recall details

• Make connections using illustrations, prior knowledge, or real-life experiences

Reinforcing the Concept

Reread the Day 1 story. Then reinforce this week's science concept by guiding a discussion about the story. Say:

Our story tells us that the moon is a big ball of rock. Does the moon always look the same? (No, it looks like it changes shape.)

Distribute the Day 2 activity and crayons. Say:

• *Point to box 1. Is the moon made of rock? Color the happy face for **yes** or the sad face for **no**.* (yes)

• *Point to box 2. The girl is looking at the moon. Does it look like a full moon from Earth? Color the happy face for **yes** or the sad face for **no**.* (no)

• *Point to box 3. Does the boy see a quarter moon? Color the happy face for **yes** or the sad face for **no**.* (yes) *We can see the half of the moon that is lit up. It is called a quarter moon.*

• *Point to box 4. Is the moon still there, even if the girl can't see it? Color the happy face for **yes** or the sad face for **no**.* (yes) *A moon you cannot see is called a dark moon.*

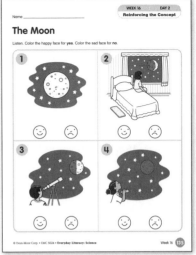

The Moon

Listen. Color the happy face for **yes**. Color the sad face for **no**.

Day 2 activity

Day 3
SKILLS

Earth Science

• Represent observations about Earth and space in a variety of ways

• Explore properties of Earth and space

• Understand that the sun, moon, and stars are objects in our sky

• Understand that the moon does not change shape

Literacy

Oral Language Development

• Respond orally to simple questions

Comprehension

• Make connections using illustrations, prior knowledge, or real-life experiences

Developing the Concept

Distribute the Day 3 activity and crayons. Then introduce the activity by saying:

You can't see the sun at night, but it is there. You can see the sun's light on the surface of the moon.

• *Point to picture 1. The surface of the moon is all lit up. What kind of moon is this?* (a full moon) *Draw a line from this full moon to the other picture that shows a full moon.*

• *Point to picture 2. We see a moon that looks like a half circle. What kind of moon is this?* (a quarter moon) *Draw a line from this quarter moon to the other picture that shows a quarter moon.*

• *Point to picture 3. The moon is in the sky, but it is dark. We cannot see the part of it that is lit up by the sun. Draw a line from the dark moon to the other picture that shows a dark moon.*

• *Point to picture 4. We see a moon that looks like a banana. What kind of moon is this?* (a crescent moon) *Draw a line from this crescent moon to the other picture that shows a crescent moon.*

The Moon

Listen and follow the directions. Draw a line to match.

Day 3 activity

Earth Science

• Represent observations about Earth and space in a variety of ways

• Explore properties of Earth and space

• Understand that the sun, moon, and stars are objects in our sky

• Understand that the moon does not change shape

Literacy

Oral Language Development

• Respond orally to simple questions

Comprehension

• Make connections using illustrations, prior knowledge, or real-life experiences

Applying the Concept

Introduce the activity by reviewing the following concept. Say:

When we look at the moon every night, it seems to change shape. We can see only the part of the moon that is lit by the sun.

Distribute the Day 4 activity and crayons. Say:

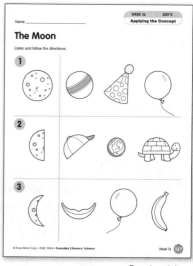

Day 4 activity

• *Look at row 1. The first picture shows a full moon. The other pictures show a beach ball, a hat, and a balloon. Look at the shapes of the pictures. Which pictures have the same shape as the moon? (beach ball, balloon) Draw a line under the pictures that have the same round shape.*

• *Look at row 2. The first picture shows a quarter moon. The other pictures show a cap, a coin, and a turtle. Look at the shapes of the pictures. Which pictures have the same half-circle shape? (cap, turtle) Draw a line under the pictures that have the same half-circle shape.*

• *Look at row 3. The first picture shows a crescent moon. The other pictures show a smile, a balloon, and a banana. Which ones have the same crescent moon shape? (smile, banana) Draw a line under the pictures that have the same crescent moon shape.*

Earth Science

• Represent observations about Earth and space in a variety of ways

• Explore properties of Earth and space

• Understand that the sun, moon, and stars are objects in our sky

• Understand that the moon does not change shape

Scientific Thinking & Inquiry

• Gather and record information through simple observations and investigations

Home–School Connection p. 138
Spanish version available (see p. 2)

Hands-on Science Activity

Reinforce this week's science concept with the following hands-on activity:

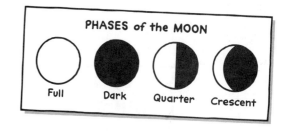

Materials: black construction paper, white or yellow construction paper, a bowl or other round traceable object, scissors, pencil

Preparation: Use the bowl to trace and cut out moon shapes from black and white (or yellow) construction paper. Cut enough pieces for each child and yourself to make each kind of moon as follows:

• **Full moon:** two white (or yellow) half circles

• **Dark moon:** two black half circles

• **Quarter moon:** one black and one white (or yellow) half circle

• **Crescent moon:** one banana-shaped white (or yellow) piece and one opposite-shaped black piece

Use your set of shapes to create a chart for children to refer to.

Activity: Give each child one pair of each kind of moon shape. Have children match pairs of moon shapes to form a full moon, a dark moon, a quarter moon, and a crescent moon. Have children refer to the chart you made to complete the activity.

Name _____

The Moon

Name _____

The Moon

Listen. Color the happy face for **yes**. Color the sad face for **no**.

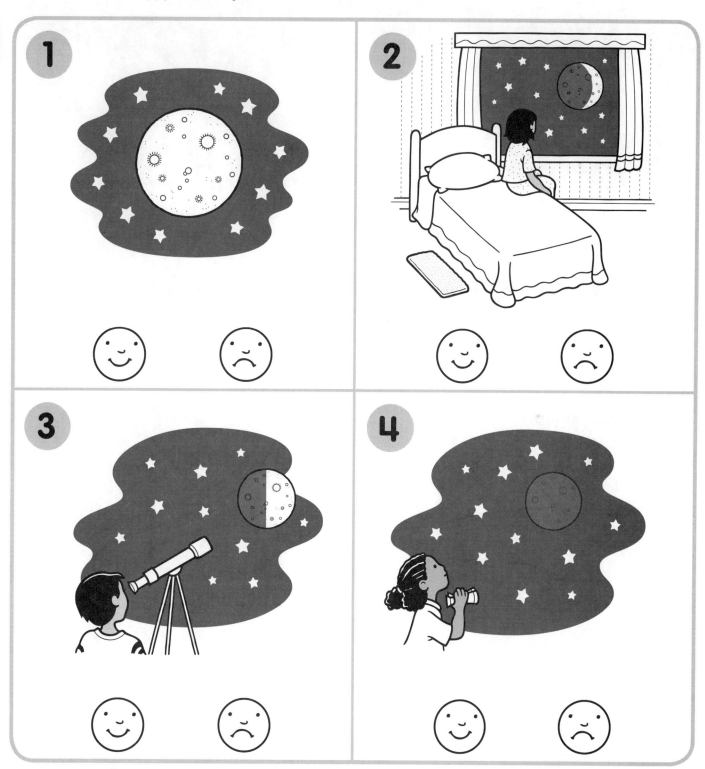

Name _____

The Moon

Listen and follow the directions. Draw a line to match.

1 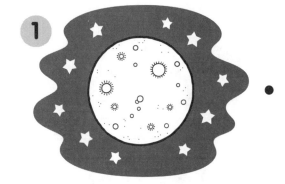 •   • 

2 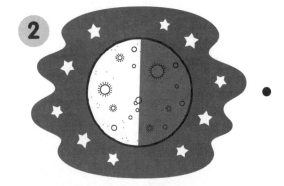 •   • 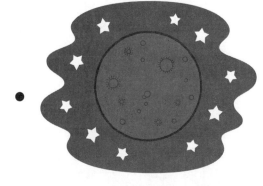

3  •   • 

4 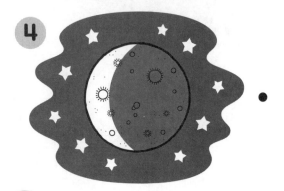 •   • 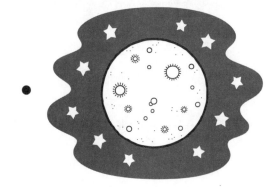

Name _____

The Moon

Listen and follow the directions.

1

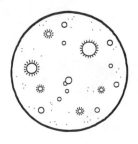 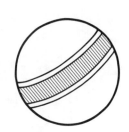  

2

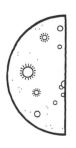  

3

Name _____

What I Learned

What to Do
Have your child look at each picture below. Ask him or her to point to the moon in each picture and tell you what kind of moon shape it is: full moon, quarter moon, crescent moon, and dark moon, and how it looks different.

Science Concept: The moon is an object in our sky that does not change shape.

To Parents
This week your child learned that the moon is an object in our sky that does not change shape.

What to Do Next
Go outside with your child and observe the moon. Then have your child draw a night scene that includes a picture of the same moon he or she just observed. Write what kind of moon it is—full moon, quarter moon, crescent moon, or dark moon.

Concept

The Earth is composed of air, land, and water.

The Earth Has Land

Science Objective:
To help children understand that Earth has areas of flat land (plains), mountains, valleys, and islands

Science Vocabulary:
Earth, flat, high, island, land, landform, low, mountain, valley

Day 1 SKILLS

Earth Science
- Represent observations about Earth and space in a variety of ways
- Explore properties of Earth and space
- Understand that the Earth is composed of air, land, and water
- Understand that the Earth has different landforms

Literacy

Oral Language Development
- Respond orally to simple questions

Comprehension
- Recall details
- Make connections using illustrations, prior knowledge, or real-life experiences
- Listen to stories being read aloud
- Make inferences and draw conclusions

Introducing the Concept

Distribute the Day 1 activity page. Point to each type of landform as you talk about it. Say:

Earth has different kinds of land. Earth has flat land. Earth has high land called mountains. Earth has low land called valleys. Earth has land called islands. Islands have water on all sides. What is the land like where you live? (children respond)

Listening to the Story

Redirect children's attention to the Day 1 page. Say: *Listen and look at the picture as I read a story about the different kinds of land on Earth.*

Visiting my relatives is fun because we travel over different types of land. My home is on flat land. My grandma's home is on a mountain. A mountain is much higher than the land around it. When we visit my grandma, we drive up, up, up. When we leave Grandma's house, we drive through a valley to my cousins' house. A valley is a low place between mountains. I like going to my cousins' house because their house is on an island, which is land that has water all around it. We drive over a bridge to get there. I sure am glad we don't have to swim!

Confirming Understanding

Distribute crayons or markers. Reinforce the science concept by asking children questions about the story. Ask:

Day 1 picture

- *What kind of land is the boy's home on?* (flat land) *Draw a blue circle around his home.*

- *What kind of land does the grandma live on?* (mountain) *What do we know about a mountain?* (It is higher than the land around it.) *Make a brown dot on the mountaintop.*

- *What kind of land did the boy drive through on the way to his cousins' house?* (valley) *Make a green line across the valley.*

- *Where do the boy's cousins live?* (on an island) *What is an island?* (Land that has water all around it.) *Color the island yellow.*

Day 2 SKILLS

Earth Science

- Represent observations about Earth and space in a variety of ways
- Explore properties of Earth and space
- Understand that the Earth is composed of air, land, and water
- Understand that the Earth has different landforms

Literacy

Oral Language Development

- Respond orally to simple questions

Comprehension

- Recall details
- Listen to stories being read aloud

Reinforcing the Concept

Reread the Day 1 story. Then reinforce this week's science concept by activating children's prior knowledge. Ask:

- *Have you ever seen a mountain? Have you ever been on a mountain?* (children respond)
- *Have you ever seen an island? Have you ever been on an island?* (children respond)

Distribute the Day 2 activity and crayons. Say:

- *Point to box 1. A mountain is land that is higher than the land around it. Does this picture show a mountain? Color the happy face for **yes** or the sad face for **no**.* (yes)
- *Point to box 2. An island is land with water on all sides. Does this picture show an island? Color the happy face for **yes** or the sad face for **no**.* (no)
- *Point to box 3. Does this land look flat? Color the happy face for **yes** or the sad face for **no**.* (yes)
- *Point to box 4. A valley is low land between mountains. Is there a valley between the mountains in this picture? Color the happy face for **yes** or the sad face for **no**.* (yes)

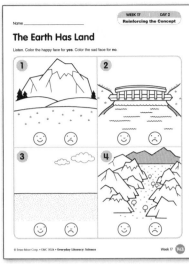

Day 2 activity

Day 3 SKILLS

Earth Science

- Represent observations about Earth and space in a variety of ways
- Explore properties of Earth and space
- Understand that the Earth is composed of air, land, and water
- Understand that the Earth has different landforms

Literacy

Oral Language Development

- Respond orally to simple questions

Comprehension

- Make connections using illustrations, prior knowledge, or real-life experiences

Applying the Concept

Introduce the activity by saying:

We are learning about four types of land: flat land, mountains, valleys, and islands. What kind of land would you like to live on? Why? (children respond)

Distribute the Day 3 activity and crayons. Say:

- *Point to picture 1. Abby lives on a farm. There is flat land all around. Draw a line from Abby to the picture that shows flat land.*
- *Point to picture 2. Rob lives high up in the mountains. It is cold there. Draw a line from Rob to the picture that shows mountains.*
- *Point to picture 3. Anthony lives on an island. It has water on all sides. Draw a line from Anthony to the picture that shows an island.*
- *Point to picture 4. Ella lives in a valley. There are mountains all around, but the land where she lives is low. Draw a line from Ella to the picture that shows a valley.*

Day 3 activity

Earth Science

- Represent observations about Earth and space in a variety of ways

- Explore properties of Earth and space

- Understand that the Earth is composed of air, land, and water

- Understand that the Earth has different landforms

Literacy

Oral Language Development

- Respond orally to simple questions

Comprehension

- Make connections using illustrations, prior knowledge, or real-life experiences

Applying the Concept

Introduce the activity by reviewing the science concept. Say:

Earth has different kinds of landforms: flat land, mountains, valleys, and islands.

Distribute the Day 4 activity and crayons. Say:

- *This picture shows the track for the Big Race! You are going to pretend that you are in the race. Can you win? Here's what you must do. Listen carefully and follow my directions.*

- *Put your crayon at the top of the mountain. You must run down the mountain to the valley below it. Draw a line down the mountain to the valley. Draw an **X** on the spot where you reach the valley.*

- *Next, you must run through the valley to the place where flat land begins. Draw a line through the valley to the flat land. Draw an **X** on the spot where you reach the flat land.*

- *Now, run across the flat land to the bridge. Draw an **X** on the bridge.*

- *To win the race, you must run across the bridge to the island. Draw a line to the island. You won! Draw a happy face on the island.*

WEEK 17   DAY 4
Applying the Concept

Name _____

The Earth Has Land

Listen. Draw a line to show the path of the Big Race.

© Evan-Moor Corp. • EMC 5024 • **Everyday Literacy: Science**   Week 17   145

Day 4 activity

Day 5
SKILLS

Earth Science

- Represent observations about Earth and space in a variety of ways

- Explore properties of Earth and space

- Understand that the Earth is composed of air, land, and water

- Understand that the Earth has different landforms

Scientific Thinking & Inquiry

- Explore physical properties of objects and materials

Hands-on Science Activity

Reinforce this week's science concept with the following hands-on activity:

Materials: sand table or sandbox, sand, shovels, containers of water

Activity: Direct children to use sand and water to make the landforms they learned about this week. First, have them build tall mountains, with low valleys in between. Then have children smooth areas of sand for the flat land. To make an island, children can pour water into a moat dug around a mound of sand. Discuss the different landscapes, and encourage children to use the terms they learned for landforms: **flat land, mountain, valley,** and **island**.

Home–School Connection p. 146
Spanish version available (see p. 2)

Name _____

The Earth Has Land

Name _____

The Earth Has Land

Listen. Color the happy face for **yes**. Color the sad face for **no**.

Name _____

The Earth Has Land

Listen. Draw lines to match the pictures.

1    •   •

2    •   •

3    •   •

4    •   •

    Everyday Literacy: Science • EMC 5024 • © Evan-Moor Corp.

Name _____

The Earth Has Land

Listen. Draw a line to show the path of the Big Race.

Name _____

What I Learned

What to Do
Have your child look at the picture below. Ask him or her to point to each landform: the flat land (plains), mountains, valley, and island. Talk about the characteristics of each one: flat, high, low, and surrounded by water.

Science Concept: The Earth is composed of air, land, and water.

To Parents
This week your child learned that Earth is composed of air, land, and water and has different landforms.

What to Do Next
Create landforms with your child using play clay. Make mountains, valleys, flat land, and islands.

Everyday Literacy: Science • EMC 5024 • © Evan-Moor Corp.

All Kinds of Rocks

Science Objective:
To help children understand that rocks can be described by their shape, size, color, and hardness

Science Vocabulary:
color, hard, jagged, rock, rough, scratch, shape, size, smooth, texture

Day 1 SKILLS

Earth Science
- Represent observations about Earth and space in a variety of ways
- Explore properties of Earth and space
- Understand that the Earth is composed of air, land, and water
- Understand that rocks have different properties

Literacy

Oral Language Development
- Respond orally to simple questions

Comprehension
- Recall details
- Make connections using illustrations, prior knowledge, or real-life experiences
- Listen to stories being read aloud
- Make inferences and draw conclusions

Introducing the Concept

Pass around several rocks for children to look at and touch. Say:

You can find rocks everywhere on Earth. Rocks come from pieces of Earth's land. But not all rocks are the same.

- *Feel these rocks. Do they all feel the same? How do they feel?* (rough, smooth, bumpy, scratchy, hard)
- *Look at these rocks. What colors are they? What shapes are they?* (children respond)

Listening to the Story

Distribute the Day 1 activity page and crayons. Say: *Listen and look at the picture as I read a story about children who collect rocks.*

Maya and Fuyu went for a walk. They found a lot of rocks! They put the rocks into bags and brought them home. Fuyu looked at the rocks' colors. She saw that some rocks had one color and some rocks had many colors. She washed off the rocks and saw even more colors! Then Maya touched the rocks. Some felt smooth and some felt rough. Some were very hard and shiny, and some were a little crumbly. One broke when Maya tapped it against the table. "That's okay," said Maya. "I just made another rock!"

Confirming Understanding

Distribute crayons. Reinforce the science concept by asking questions about the story. Ask:

- *Are all rocks the same?* (no) *Do some rocks have one color?* (yes) *Circle a rock that has one color. Do some rocks have more than one color?* (yes) *Make a red dot on a rock that has more than one color.*
- *Do all rocks feel the same?* (No, some are smooth, some rough.) *Make a blue dot on a rock that looks smooth. Make a green dot on a rock that looks rough.*
- *Can a rock break?* (yes) *Make an **X** on the broken rock in Maya's hand.*

Day 1 picture

Reinforcing the Concept

Reread the Day 1 story. Then reinforce this week's science concept by guiding a discussion about the story. Say:

In our story, Fuyu and Maya learned about rocks.

- *Tell me two things they learned about rocks. (Some have one color and some have many colors; rocks are different shapes and sizes, etc.)*

Distribute the Day 2 activity and crayons. Say:

- *Point to box 1. The girls collected a lot of rocks. Do all the rocks in the bag look the same? Color the happy face for **yes** or the sad face for **no**.* (no)

- *Point to box 2. The girl is holding a rock. Do you think the rock feels rough? Color the happy face for **yes** or the sad face for **no**.* (yes)

- *Point to box 3. There are two rocks in the water. Are the rocks the same size? Color the happy face for **yes** or the sad face for **no**.* (no)

- *Point to box 4. This rock fell on the ground. Did it break? Color the happy face for **yes** or the sad face for **no**.* (yes)

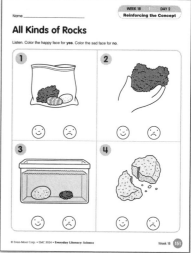

Day 2 activity

Applying the Concept

Distribute the Day 3 activity and crayons. Then introduce the activity by saying:

We can learn more about rocks by looking at their shapes, their sizes, and their textures. Let's look at the rocks on this page and talk about them.

- *Point to row 1. Point to the first rock. Do you think this rock feels rough or smooth? (smooth) Now look at the rocks next to it. Circle the other rock that looks smooth.*

- *Point to row 2. Point to the first rock. Does this rock have one color? (yes) Now look at the rocks next to it. Circle the other rock that has only one color.*

- *Point to row 3. Point to the first rock. Does this rock look round? (yes) Now look at the rocks next to it. Circle the other rock that looks round.*

- *Point to row 4. Point to the first rock. Is this rock broken or whole? (broken) Now look at the rocks next to it. Circle the other rock that is broken.*

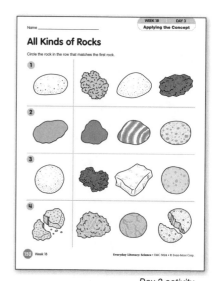

Day 3 activity

Day 4
SKILLS

Earth Science

• Represent observations about Earth and space in a variety of ways

• Explore properties of Earth and space

• Understand that the Earth is composed of air, land, and water

• Understand that rocks have different properties

Literacy

Oral Language Development

• Respond orally to simple questions

Comprehension

• Make connections using illustrations, prior knowledge, or real-life experiences

• Make inferences and draw conclusions

Applying the Concept

Introduce the activity by saying:

It's fun to look closely at rocks. You can learn many things about them. Have you ever found a rock you liked a lot? Tell me about it. (children respond)

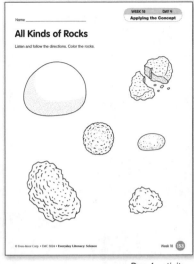

Day 4 activity

Distribute the Day 4 activity and crayons. Say:

There are different kinds of rocks on this page. They look big and small, smooth and rough, round and jagged. Listen carefully and follow my directions.

- *Put your finger on the rock that looks big and smooth. Color it blue.*
- *Put your finger on the rock that looks rough and round. Color it purple.*
- *Put your finger on the rock that looks small and smooth. Color it black.*
- *Put your finger on the rock that looks big and rough. Color it red.*
- *Put your finger on the rock that is broken. Color the broken pieces of rock brown.*
- *Put your finger on the rock that is small and jagged. Color it orange.*

Day 5
SKILLS

Earth Science

• Represent observations about Earth and space in a variety of ways

• Explore properties of Earth and space

• Understand that the Earth is composed of air, land, and water

• Understand that rocks have different properties

Scientific Thinking & Inquiry

• Gather and record information through simple observations and investigations

Hands-on Science Activity

Reinforce this week's science concept with the following hands-on activity:

Materials: a paper lunch bag for each child

Activity: Take children on a nature walk and have them collect rocks and place them in their paper bags. Then have children go back to the classroom and sort their rocks into categories such as big, small, rough, smooth, one color, and many colors, etc. Allow children to place one rock in the sink and run water on it and observe its colors.

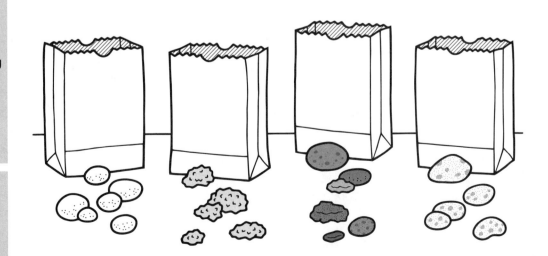

Home–School Connection p. 154
Spanish version available (see p. 2)

Name _____

All Kinds of Rocks

Name _____

All Kinds of Rocks

Listen. Color the happy face for **yes**. Color the sad face for **no**.

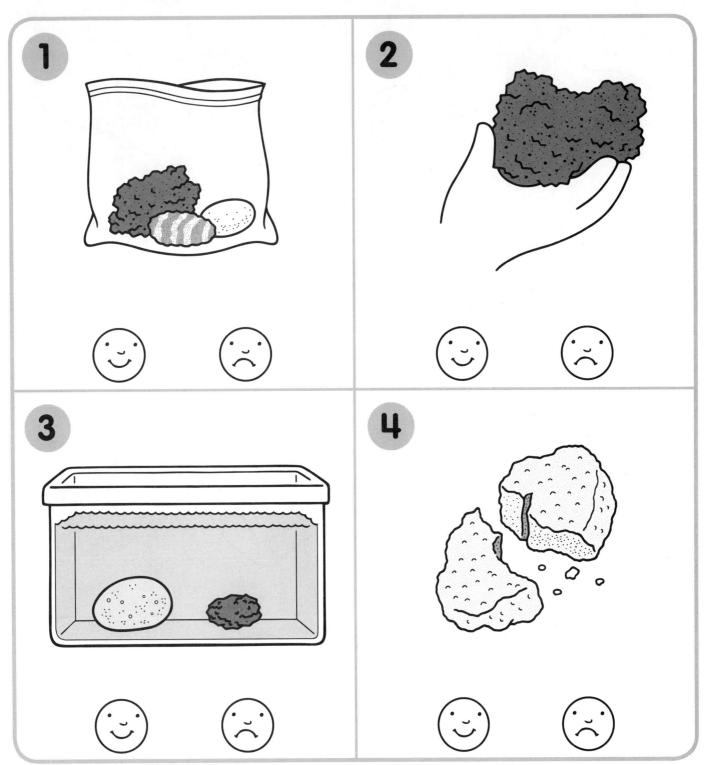

Name _____

All Kinds of Rocks

Circle the rock in the row that matches the first rock.

1

 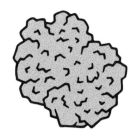 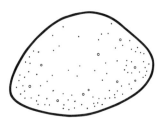 

2

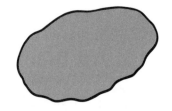   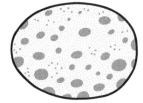

3

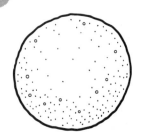  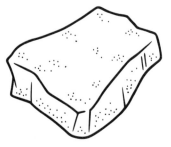 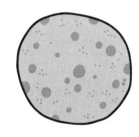

4

 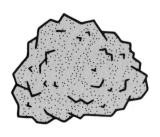  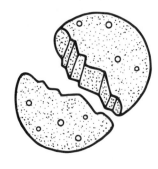

Everyday Literacy: Science • EMC 5024 • © Evan-Moor Corp.

Name _____

All Kinds of Rocks

Listen and follow the directions. Color the rocks.

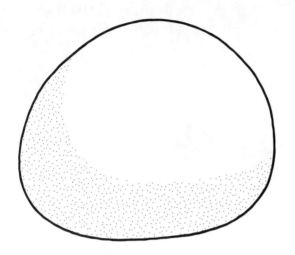

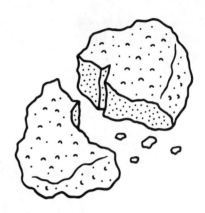

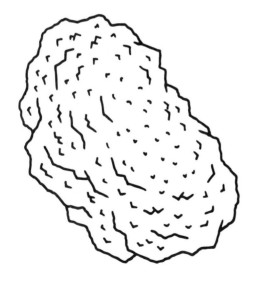

Name _____

What I Learned

What to Do

Have your child look at the picture below. Ask him or her to tell you what things he or she can learn about rocks. For example, a rock's color, its shape, its size, how it feels, and its hardness. Then have your child point out each rock's different attributes.

Science Concept: Earth has land, and rocks are part of the land.

To Parents

This week your child learned that rocks can be described by their physical properties: shape, size, color, and hardness.

What to Do Next

Go on a rock hunt with your child to collect rocks of different shapes, sizes, colors, and textures. Then have him or her sort the rocks by shape, size, color, and texture.

Concept

The Earth is composed of air, land, and water.

Air Is Everywhere

Science Objective:
To help children understand that air is everywhere, even though we cannot see it

Science Vocabulary:
air, blow, gust, move, wind

Day 1
SKILLS

Earth Science
- Represent observations about Earth and space in a variety of ways
- Explore properties of Earth and space
- Understand that the Earth is composed of air, land, and water
- Understand that air is everywhere

Literacy

Oral Language Development
- Respond orally to simple questions

Comprehension
- Recall details
- Make connections using illustrations, prior knowledge, or real-life experiences
- Listen to stories being read aloud
- Make inferences and draw conclusions

Introducing the Concept

Show children an uninflated balloon and have them watch as you blow it up. Then say:

When I blew up the balloon, air went into it. You can't see the air, but you know it is there because the balloon got bigger.

- *Watch as I let the air out of the balloon.* Release the air slowly. *Can you see the air?* (no) *How do you know it is coming out?* (The balloon is getting smaller.)

- *Now blow on your hand. What do you feel?* (breath, a puff of air) *Can you see it?* (no) *You can't see the air, but you know it is there because you can feel it. You can also feel air move when the wind blows.*

Listening to the Story

Distribute the Day 1 activity page to each child. Say: *Listen and look at the picture as I read a story about a boy and his dad at a park on a windy day.*

Wesley and his dad went to the park on a windy day. "Wow! The air is really moving today. You can't see it, but you sure can feel it!" said his dad. Wesley saw a clown blowing up a balloon. It got bigger and bigger. "How is he making the balloon so big?" asked Wesley. His dad told him that the clown was blowing air into the balloon. All of a sudden, a big gust of wind blew one of the clown's balloons away. Wesley chased after it and caught it. He brought it back to his dad and said, "You were right! The air is really moving today, but I'm moving faster!"

Confirming Understanding

Distribute crayons or markers. Reinforce the science concept by asking children questions about the story. Say:

- *Wesley watched the clown's balloon get bigger and bigger. What made the balloon get bigger?* (The clown was blowing air into the balloon.) *Make a purple dot on the clown's balloon.*

- *What made the clown's balloon blow away?* (the wind) *The wind is moving air. Color something that the air is moving.*

Day 1 picture

Day 2
SKILLS

Earth Science

- Represent observations about Earth and space in a variety of ways
- Explore properties of Earth and space
- Understand that the Earth is composed of air, land, and water
- Understand that air is everywhere

Literacy

Oral Language Development

- Respond orally to simple questions

Comprehension

- Recall details
- Listen to stories being read aloud
- Make inferences and draw conclusions

Reinforcing the Concept

Reread the Day 1 story. Then reinforce this week's science concept by guiding a discussion about the story. Say:

Air is everywhere, even though we cannot see it. We can feel air when it is moving or blowing.

- *How did Wesley know that the air was moving?* (The wind blew away the clown's balloon; his dad told him.)

Distribute the Day 2 activity and crayons. Say:

- *Point to box 1. The wind is moving air. Did the wind blow away the clown's balloon? Color the happy face for **yes** or the sad face for **no**.* (yes)

- *Point to box 2. Is there air in the balloon? Color the happy face for **yes** or the sad face for **no**.* (yes) *How do you know?* (The balloon is big.)

- *Point to box 3. Air is everywhere. Can you see air? Color the happy face for **yes** or the sad face for **no**.* (no)

- *Point to box 4. Air is everywhere. Can you feel air move? Color the happy face for **yes** or the sad face for **no**.* (yes)

Day 2 activity

Day 3
SKILLS

Earth Science

- Represent observations about Earth and space in a variety of ways
- Explore properties of Earth and space
- Understand that the Earth is composed of air, land, and water
- Understand that air is everywhere

Literacy

Oral Language Development

- Respond orally to simple questions

Comprehension

- Make connections using illustrations, prior knowledge, or real-life experiences
- Make inferences and draw conclusions

Applying the Concept

To introduce the activity, guide a discussion that helps children recall the Day 1 story. Say:

Although we cannot see air, we know it is there. We can see air make a balloon get bigger. Did you ever pop a balloon? What happened? (It made a loud noise.) *That's right, all the air rushing out of the balloon at once makes a loud noise.*

Distribute the Day 3 activity and crayons. Say:

- *Point to the picture of the girl holding a balloon that does not have any air in it. How does the balloon look?* (small and flat) *Draw a line from the picture to number 1.*

- *Now point to the picture of the girl blowing air into the balloon. How has the balloon changed?* (It got bigger and rounder.) *Draw a line from the picture to number 2.*

- *Now point to the picture of the girl holding the balloon after it is blown up. The girl tied the balloon to keep the air inside it. How does the balloon look?* (round, full) *Draw a line from the picture to number 3.*

- *Now point to the picture of the girl holding the balloon after it popped. How has the balloon changed?* (The air went out; The balloon is in pieces.) *Draw a line from the picture to number 4.*

Day 3 activity

Everyday Literacy: Science • EMC 5024 • © Evan-Moor Corp.

Earth Science
• Represent observations about Earth and space in a variety of ways
• Explore properties of Earth and space
• Understand that the Earth is composed of air, land, and water
• Understand that air is everywhere

Literacy
Oral Language Development
• Respond orally to simple questions
Comprehension
• Make inferences and draw conclusions
• Make connections using illustrations, prior knowledge, or real-life experiences

Extending the Concept

Introduce the activity by saying:

Air is all around us. Have you ever felt the air move? Tell me about it. (children respond)

Distribute the Day 4 activity and crayons. Say:

• *Point to picture 1. It shows a ball that is not blown up. What will make the ball get bigger?* (blowing air into it) *Air fills the ball and makes it get bigger. Draw a line to the picture that shows the ball filled with air.*

• *Point to picture 2. It shows a kite lying on the ground. Have you ever flown a kite?* (children respond) *The wind lifts a kite into the air. The wind is moving air. Draw a line to the picture that shows the kite flying in the air.*

• *Point to picture 3. It shows a pile of leaves on the ground. Have you ever seen the wind blow a pile of leaves around?* (children respond) *The wind is moving air. The wind moves the leaves. Draw a line to the picture that shows the wind moving the leaves.*

• *Point to picture 4. It shows a closed window. Have you ever opened a window and felt the air blow in?* (children respond) *Air moves. When you open a window and air blows in, it moves the curtains. Draw a line to the picture that shows the wind moving the curtains.*

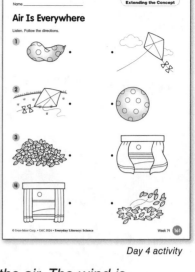

Day 4 activity

Earth Science
• Represent observations about Earth and space in a variety of ways
• Explore properties of Earth and space
• Understand that the Earth is composed of air, land, and water
• Understand that air is everywhere

Scientific Thinking & Inquiry
• Gather and record information through simple observations and investigations

Hands-on Science Activity

Reinforce this week's science concept with the following hands-on activity:

Materials: one bottle of bubble solution and one wand for each child

Activity: Conduct the activity in an outdoor space. Model how to blow a bubble. Then say:

You blow air from your body into the bubble. The air from your body makes the bubble big and round.

Then give each child a bottle of bubble solution and a wand and allow children to spend time blowing bubbles. Then say:

When the wind blows, it moves your bubbles. Wind is moving air.

Have half of the children blow bubbles as the other half chases the bubbles. Then have children switch groups.

Home–School Connection p. 162
Spanish version available (see p. 2)

Name _____

Air Is Everywhere

Everyday Literacy: Science • EMC 5024 • © Evan-Moor Corp.

Name _____

Air Is Everywhere

Listen. Color the happy face for **yes**. Color the sad face for **no**.

Name _____

Air Is Everywhere

Listen. Then draw a line from the picture to **1**, **2**, **3**, or **4**.

•   • 1

•   • 2

•   • 3

•   • 4

Everyday Literacy: Science • EMC 5024 • © Evan-Moor Corp.

Name _____

Air Is Everywhere

Listen. Follow the directions.

1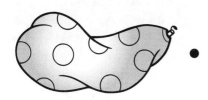

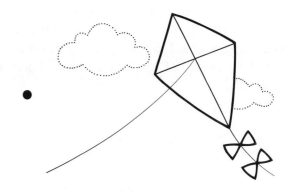

2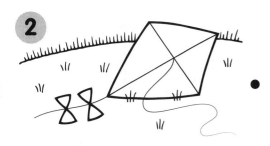

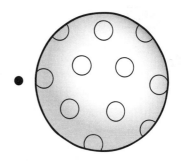

3

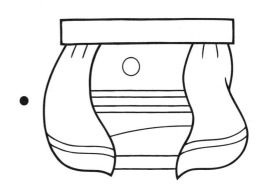

4

Name _____

What I Learned

What to Do
Have your child look at the picture below. Ask him or her to point to things that show moving air, such as leaves blowing, kite flying, and trees moving. Tell your child that we know air is everywhere because we see what moving air does. Then have your child color the picture.

WEEK 19

Home–School Connection

Science Concept: The Earth is composed of air, land, and water.

To Parents
This week your child learned that air is everywhere, even though we cannot see it.

What to Do Next
Blow bubbles in an outdoor space with your child. Discuss how you blow air from your body into the bubbles. Point out that the air moves the bubbles around.

Everyday Literacy: Science • EMC 5024 • © Evan-Moor Corp.

How's the Weather?

Science Objective:
To help children understand that there are different types of weather

Science Vocabulary:
cloudy, rainy, snowy, sunny, weather, windy

Day 1 SKILLS

Earth Science

- Represent observations about Earth and space in a variety of ways
- Explore properties of Earth and space
- Understand that weather changes from day to day and across seasons
- Understand that there are different types of weather

Literacy

Oral Language Development

- Respond orally to simple questions

Comprehension

- Recall details
- Make connections using illustrations, prior knowledge, or real-life experiences
- Listen to stories being read aloud
- Make inferences and draw conclusions

Introducing the Concept

Begin by activating prior knowledge about different types of weather. Ask:

- *What is the weather like today? Is it sunny? cloudy? warm? cold?* (children respond)
- *There are many types of weather. The weather can be sunny, cloudy, rainy, windy, or snowy. It can change from one day to the next. What was the weather like yesterday?* (children respond)
- *What is your favorite type of weather?* (children respond)

Listening to the Story

Distribute the Day 1 activity page to each child. Say: *Listen and look at the picture as I read a story about a boy who watches the weather.*

David's mother wakes him up. It is time to get dressed. David doesn't know what to wear because he doesn't know what the weather is like. Yesterday the weather was sunny. David wore his blue shirt, shorts, and sandals. What will the weather be like today? Will it be sunny, rainy, foggy, cloudy, or snowy? David looks out his bedroom window. Now he knows what to wear. David puts on pants, a sweatshirt, and warm socks. Then he puts on his raincoat and steps into his rain boots. David is ready for rainy weather!

Confirming Understanding

Distribute crayons or markers. Reinforce the science concept by asking children questions about the story. Ask:

- *Why did David look out his bedroom window?* (to see what the weather was like) *Make a green dot on David's window.*
- *What did David see when he looked out his window?* (rainy weather) *Color one of the raindrops blue.*
- *What clothes did David wear on the rainy day?* (pants, sweatshirt, warm socks, raincoat, boots) *Make a yellow dot on David's raincoat. Make a red dot on David's boots.*

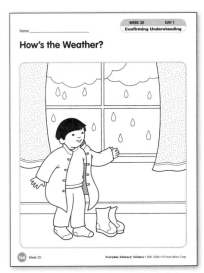

Day 1 picture

Earth Science

- Represent observations about Earth and space in a variety of ways
- Explore properties of Earth and space
- Understand that weather changes from day to day and across seasons
- Understand that there are different types of weather

Literacy

Oral Language Development

- Respond orally to simple questions

Comprehension

- Recall details
- Make connections using illustrations, prior knowledge, or real-life experiences

Reinforcing the Concept

Reread the Day 1 story. Then reinforce this week's science concept by guiding a discussion about the story. Say:

Our story was about how the weather changes. Why did David look outside before he got dressed in the morning? (to see what the weather was like so he could decide what to wear)

- *What did David see?* (rain) *What had the weather been like the day before?* (sunny)

Distribute the Day 2 activity and crayons. Say:

- *Point to box 1. David wears a shirt, shorts, and sandals on a sunny day. Does this show David on a sunny day? Color the happy face for* **yes** *or the sad face for* **no***.* (yes)

- *Point to box 2. David wears pants, a sweatshirt, warm socks, a raincoat, and rain boots on a rainy day. Does this show David on a rainy day? Color the happy face for* **yes** *or the sad face for* **no***.* (no)

- *Point to box 3. Can the weather be sunny on Monday and rainy on Tuesday? Color the happy face for* **yes** *or the sad face for* **no***.* (yes)

- *Point to box 4. Look at the picture. What type of weather do you see?* (snow) *Should David wear his shorts and sandals? Color the happy face for* **yes** *or the sad face for* **no***.* (no)

Day 2 activity

Earth Science

- Understand that weather changes from day to day and across seasons
- Understand that there are different types of weather

Literacy

Oral Language Development

- Use descriptive language
- Respond orally to simple questions

Comprehension

- Make connections using illustrations, prior knowledge, or real-life experiences
- Make inferences and draw conclusions

Reinforcing the Concept

Distribute the Day 3 activity and crayons. Then introduce the activity by saying:

Weather changes from day to day. It can be sunny, rainy, cloudy, windy, or snowy.

- *Point to box 1. What kind of weather do you see?* (snowy) *How do you know it's snowy?* (snow falling, snow on tree, snowman) *Do you think it is warm outside or cold outside?* (cold) *Color the snowman's hat red.*

- *Point to box 2. What kind of weather do you see?* (sunny) *How do you know it's sunny?* (sun in sky) *Do you think it is warm outside or cold outside?* (warm) *Color the sun yellow.*

- *Point to box 3. What kind of weather do you see?* (rainy) *How do you know it's rainy?* (rain falling from clouds in sky, puddles on ground) *Color the rain cloud gray.*

- *Point to box 4. What kind of weather do you see?* (windy) *How do you know it's windy?* (tree swaying, leaves blowing, kite flying) *Color the kite blue.*

Day 3 activity

Earth Science

- Explore properties of Earth and space
- Understand that weather changes from day to day and across seasons
- Understand that there are different types of weather

Literacy

Comprehension

- Make connections using illustrations, prior knowledge, or real-life experiences

Applying the Concept

Distribute the Day 4 activity and crayons. Then introduce the activity by saying:

Weather changes from day to day. People wear clothes that help them to stay cool or warm or dry in different kinds of weather.

- *Point to picture 1. Michael is wearing his long pants, jacket, and scarf because the weather is windy. The wind blows the leaves off the tree. Draw a line from Michael to the picture that shows wind.*

- *Point to picture 2. Tina is wearing her raincoat and holding her umbrella because the weather is rainy. Draw a line from Tina to the picture that shows rain.*

- *Point to picture 3. David is wearing shorts and a T-shirt because the weather is hot and sunny. Draw a line from David to the picture that shows sunshine.*

- *Point to picture 4. Isabella is wearing a snowsuit and boots because the weather is cold and snowy. Draw a line from Isabella to the picture that shows snow.*

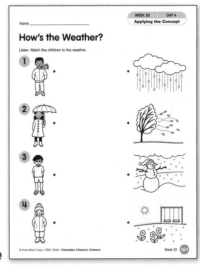

Day 4 activity

Earth Science

- Represent observations about Earth and space in a variety of ways
- Understand that weather changes from day to day and across seasons
- Understand that there are different types of weather

Literacy

Oral Language Development

- Use descriptive language

Scientific Thinking & Inquiry

- Gather and record information through simple observations and investigations

Hands-on Science Activity

Reinforce this week's science concept with the following hands-on activity:

Materials: paper plate, index card, brad, markers

Preparation: Make a weather dial by drawing lines to divide the plate into five sections. Draw a symbol for a sunny day, cloudy day, rainy day, windy day, and snowy day in each section. Cut a small arrow from an index card and poke a brad through the arrow and the middle of the plate to make a dial.

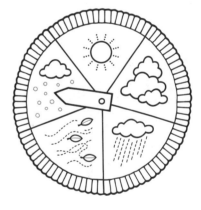

Activity: Each day for a week, have children look out the window and describe the weather. Choose a child to move the dial to indicate today's weather. Discuss the idea of dressing appropriately for the weather. Then have children point out how they dressed for today's weather.

Home–School Connection p. 170
Spanish version available (see p. 2)

Name _____

How's the Weather?

Name _____

How's the Weather?

Listen. Color the happy face for **yes**. Color the sad face for **no**.

Name _____

How's the Weather?

Listen. Follow the directions.

Name _____

How's the Weather?

Listen. Match the children to the weather.

Name _____

What I Learned

What to Do

Have your child tell you what the weather is like in the picture below. Then discuss what the boy will probably wear on this rainy day. Talk about what he might wear if it were sunny, snowy, or windy. Then have your child color the picture.

WEEK 20

Home–School Connection

Science Concept: Weather changes from day to day and across seasons.

To Parents

This week your child learned that there are different types of weather.

What to Do Next

Play a guessing game with your child. Say: *I'm getting dressed, and I'm wearing shorts and a T-shirt. What is the weather like?* (sunny) Continue with other types of weather.

Answer Key

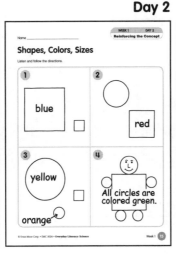
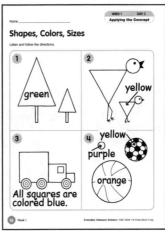
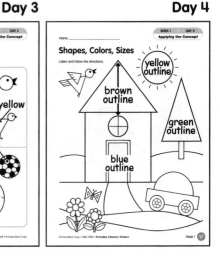

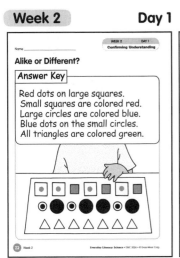
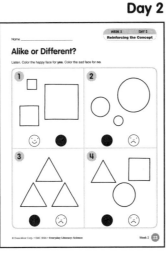
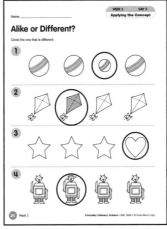
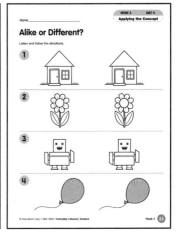

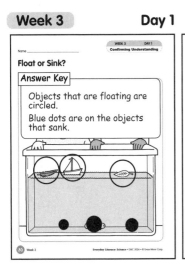

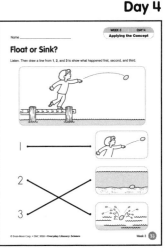

Week 4

Day 1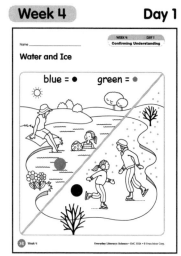

Day 2

Day 3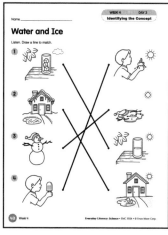

Day 4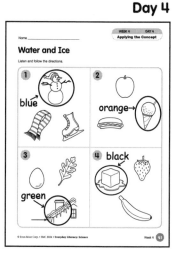

Week 5

Day 1

Day 2

Day 3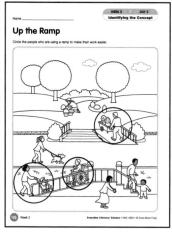

Day 4

Week 6

Day 1

Day 2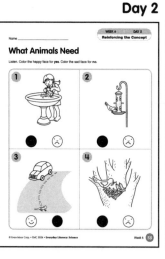

Day 3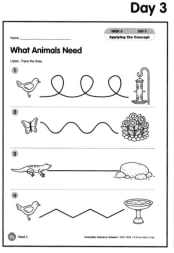

Day 4

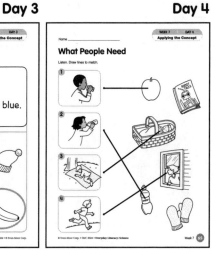

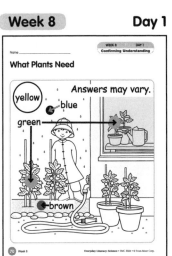

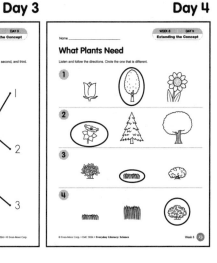

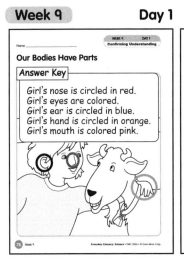

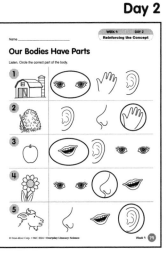

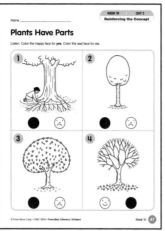
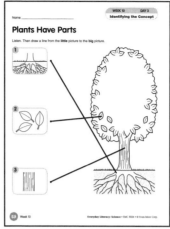
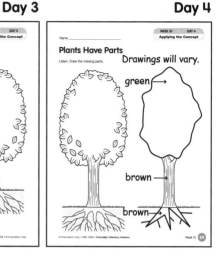

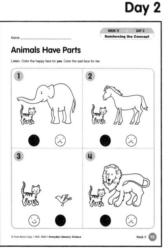
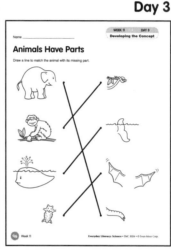
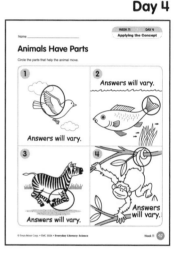

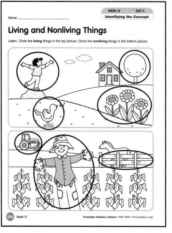

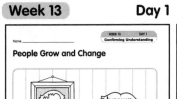

People Grow and Change

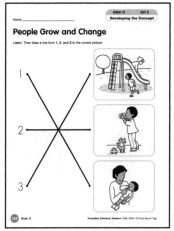

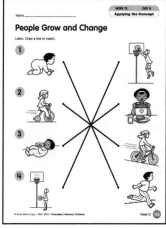

We Need the Sun

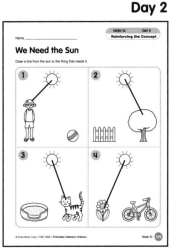

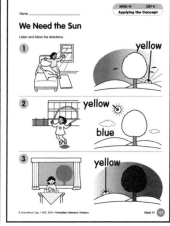

Day and Night

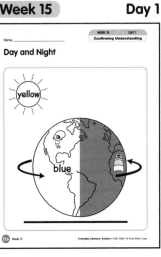

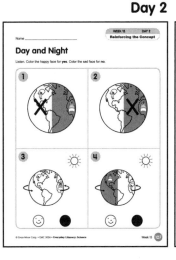

Week 16

Day 1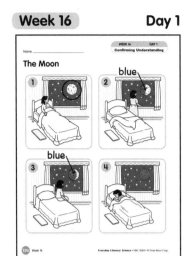

Day 2

Day 3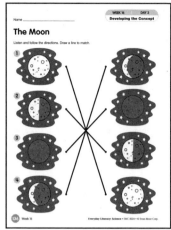

Day 4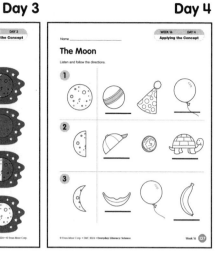

Week 17

Day 1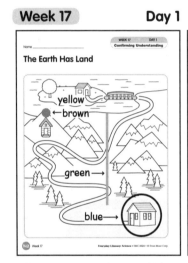

Day 2

Day 3

Day 4

Week 18

Day 1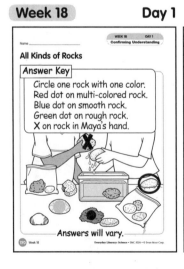

Day 2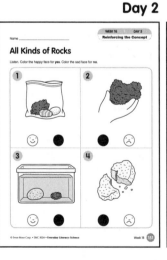

Day 3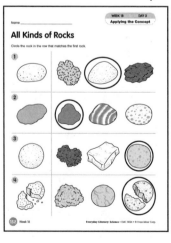

Day 4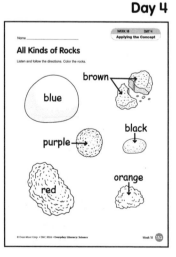